# Gracious Gifts...
# Expressions
# of the Divine

Dearest Kendra,
 May this book shower you with
grace and peace. It is never too late
to follow any dream. Believe.
 With love and gratitude,
 Sonya Haramis, M. Ed.

136

136

41YMQT0020QF

| | |
|---|---|
| Title | Gracious Gifts. . . Expressions of the Divine |
| Condition | Good |
| Location | Row G11 Bay 9 Item 136 |
| Source | GSB |
| SKU | 41YMQT0020QF |
| ASIN | 0976224704 |
| Code | 9780976224709 |
| Employee | david |
| Date Added | 9/21/2023 12.22.29 PM |

# Gracious Gifts...
## Expressions
### of the Divine

Sonya Haramis, M. Ed.

Published by
*Peace of the Dreamer*

Peace of the Dreamer
www.peaceofthedreamer.com

Library of Congress Control Number:  2004195490

ISBN: 0-9762247-0-4

Printed in the United States of America

# Contents

## The Parables...

# Preface

~

*Gracious Gifts...Expressions of the Divine* is a series of devotional parables and visions with the Divine, the Master, the Mother, Archangel Gabriel, and other angels, through the eyes of the Dreamer. You may read *Gracious Gifts... Expressions of the Divine* a chapter at a time for comfort and inspiration, or in its entirety, deepening your relationship with the Divine.

Perhaps you will feel guided to answers to the eternal questions we all ask, as you read this book. Read with your soul and heart instead of your mind to uncover the secrets hidden within the parables.

Journey with the Dreamer to places unseen but known to the soul. Walk with the Dreamer and see the Divine, touch His angelic realm, and meet the Master. Be comforted by the Mother and feel Her serenity as you pore over the words.

Allow yourself to be transported to the healing Source of these visions, for all of us are the Dreamer.

It is my prayer that these parables will comfort you and offer you hope, strength, and peace, and bring you closer to the Master and His angelic realm.

Join the Dreamer in a guided journey Home and return to the place where all things begin and where we will all return. Let go... surrender to the gracious gifts that await you.

# Introduction

~

In the distance the Dreamer noticed an enormous and mysterious mountain and slowly but methodically walked towards it. A vision came to the Dreamer. She felt she had once been left on the mountain long ago, by her elders to learn about her life path. Deep within her vision, the Dreamer walked with unsure steps and began to climb the mountain. When she felt too tired to take one more step, she clung to the mountain that seemed to beg for her life, with all of her strength.

Knowing she was desperate for help, her elders visited her in spirit and whispered secrets of the universe in her ear, to give her hope and help her hang on. Her elders left her there long ago for a quest, not only for vision and healing, but also for wisdom and strength. If she endured this quest, she would forever have the gift of vision. Only alone could she discover the secrets of creation, the stars, the wind, the elements, Nature, and humanity. And only on this mountain would they reveal their truth to her.

The Dreamer clutched the great mountain as her hand gripped her heart. She thought, "Surely I will die." Yet with a strange strength she held on, gripping the pulsating earth beneath her.

As she was about to let go, she felt the mountain begin to move and breathe. Its veins pulsated with the rhythm of her breath and understood the feelings pouring through her like open wounds waiting to be cleansed and healed. When the Dreamer's grip could no longer hold, the mountain enveloped her, sealing her within its surprising warmth. What had been hard and cold became gentle, warm, and loving. The fierce and frightening mountain became her haven. She was immobilized yet felt free of her body, and at one with her spirit. "Was this mountain part of her soul?" she wondered.

The Dreamer's elders were again with her, welcoming her into their sacred place without speaking a word. Everything within the mountain was alive. The inner chamber of the mountain rock was full of light. The Dreamer began to see beautiful colors within the mountain. The colors passed through her in blue, green mists, while white stars and flashes of light flew by her. She was fascinated and mesmerized by what she saw and felt, and knew she was home.

As the Dreamer inhaled, she smelled a smoke her soul recognized as the breath of the mountain, and she exhaled her breath as an offering. As she inhaled again, she became part of the inner mountain and of all that had gone before her. She was alive and invigorated as never before.

The wind whipped around her and whispered Divine words into her expectant ears. She tilted her head back and surrendered to the moment. She could hear the beating of drums in the distance. "To what land had she come? Could she stay?" she wondered.

She journeyed deeper into the center of the mountain following her elders and saw them sit in a circle. They invited her to join them. They sat in silence around the great fire and listened to the secrets of the universe that crackled skyward. She thought it was strange yet wonderful that in the belly of the mountain, her heart beat to its rhythm. The elders bowed their heads and stared deeply into the fire, waiting for visions.

She, too, stared deeply into the fire, and as she did, her eyes changed color. What were once brown eyes became clear green with hints of firelight. The drumbeat grew louder and louder until it silenced the noise within the Dreamer. Then all fell silent. Her elders and she shared each other's gaze. New lines and expressions had formed on already magnificent faces. They knew she had met the silence and had been transformed by it. The blood on her hands from gripping onto the mountain for her life had disappeared and her desperation was transformed into bliss. She became one with all of the elements, who would guard her forever.

After a long time in deep meditation, the Dreamer suddenly felt something move in her hand. As she opened her eyes, in her hand was a baby blue bird, timid yet trusting the Dreamer. She held the baby blue bird gently and with much love. The Dreamer stroked its fragile body and wings and fed it seeds she gathered miraculously from the earth around her. As the blue bird ate, it began to flutter its wings, and grew stronger and bigger. The little bird did not yet know of its wings and therefore didn't know it could fly.

The Dreamer fell asleep while protecting her new little friend. When she awoke, she found herself outside and at the peak of the mountain, surrounded by her elders. She looked below her and saw others who did not have the courage or faith to surrender and continue on their journey up the mountain. They had become frozen in the eternal agony of climbing.

Because she held on long enough, and survived all the pain she had endured to get there, the mountain became the Dreamer's refuge, as well as the place she could take flight from.

"Well done, Dreamer," said the Chief Elder. "Because you survived your quest, and surrendered to your faith and courage, you will now receive many visions you are to share with the world. Tell them as the storyteller you are, for it will be easier for others to accept your visions as story rather than Truth. But in their hearts they will know what you write is the Truth, and they will follow you up the mountain."

The Dreamer now knew that her life's work was to share her forthcoming visions of healing and hope with all who would listen.

"Dreamer, you must write about your visions, for they will offer comfort and hope to many," continued the elder.

The Dreamer's greatest wish was to fulfill her life's work and help heal others. Reading her mind and heart, the elder gave the Dreamer an ancient writing tablet and pen, looked deeply in her eyes, and infused instructions upon her soul.

"Dreamer, it is time for you to dream..."

# The Parables...

# Chapter One

~

# *Gifts*

The Dreamer sat down beside the Master on a stone bench as He held her hand. Humbled to be in His presence, she bowed her head and closed her eyes for a moment. She felt His hand radiate. It was strong, kind, massive, and powerful. The Dreamer felt her entire being transformed from the touch of His hand. He stood up and she followed, knowing not where they were going. They were leaving the stone bench behind, yet it would await their return. They began to float, and then fly, or was He moving all things around them, she wondered.

The sky, Heaven, was first white, then pale pink, then blue. The Dreamer knew they were in a sacred place. Silence. She felt her breath move through her body. They were surrounded by blue clouds, which hung in the air like blessed smoke.

The Master sat down and motioned the Dreamer with His hand to do the same. They sat facing each other. The Master closed His eyes and as He did, the Dreamer followed. Great vision came to her, yet she knew it was His. Meditation.

As the Dreamer settled herself, the Master's voice resonated in her soul and in her mind. He began to reveal many things. In His hand He held a small, clear, gold pyramid, which glimmered in His light. He held it out to the Dreamer and put it in her hand. It felt hot in her hand and she saw that it held many visions. Secrets. She knew the people she saw within the golden, tiny pyramid, yet they could not see her. She held it for a while, and then gave it back to the Master.

He then offered the Dreamer a gold locket, a heart. This He held up and gazed at intently before He gave it to her. As she held it she quickly opened it, eager to see what was hidden inside. She saw the same people she saw in the pyramid, but they could still not see her. The Master told her to keep it and He put its golden chain around her neck.

Then the Master lit a candle. The Dreamer could not see the base of the candle, only its lit crown. It was a white pillar reaching through Heaven. She held both the Master's hands around this great white candle and could see Him through it. The locket then grew and became an armor of gold, wrapped around her entire body.

The Master blew the flame across to her. It ignited her third eye and at once a fierce wind blew by her ears. Her hair raced in the mighty wind of the Master's breath. The flame continued piercing through her third eye, directed by the Master's breath. Then the wind and the breath paused and changed direction. The Master looked at her and smiled. His power and love were extraordinary.

The Master took out of His sacred pouch a ruby. It glistened like no other stone the Dreamer had ever seen. The Master held it up in both His hands and filled it with His light and love. He smiled at her. As she gazed into the ruby, she saw herself. What she saw she loved. The Master extended His hands to her and directed her in thought.

The Dreamer held both her hands under His and as she did, the ruby bled. Her hands were covered in the ruby liquid, but she was not afraid. Her hands were burned yet they didn't hurt. The ruby liquid poured into the flame and there it disappeared. The Master held it there for her to see for quite some time. Soon she could see no more.

When the Master knew that the Dreamer had grown weary, the stone bench appeared. Still holding her hand, He led her to it. She fell asleep, lost in a trance of the miraculous. When she awakened, the Master and the Dreamer were seated on His bench as they had been before. He smiled at her.

The flame still burned, the Dreamer's coat of gold remained, and the sacred ruby became her armor just as the locket had. For the Master had bestowed His gifts in one moment. Illumination.

# Chapter Two

~

## *The Chariot*

The Master spoke, "Listen to me as I tell you great and true stories. Listen with your heart and you will know the truth. Listen in the wind, the secrets rest there for all, but only few can hear. There are stories more ancient than even before Creation, and these I will tell you now.

"Long ago, I rode my chariot in the great wind to the farthest reaches of the universe and the Divine strength and power were with me. The gold vessel carried me with its mighty weight, and its brightness was blinding yet illuminating. Only I was allowed to ride it. Only I could steer the mighty horses blazing through Heaven, for they, too, had earned the right to be there. Only my direction would they follow and only my voice could they hear. They knew not where they were going, but knew they must follow where I led.

"The chariot ride initiated all things, and set eternity into motion. Once I blazed the path, all could follow if they so chose. My journey led me to places not yet created. I learned that one had to choose between the light and the dark. Both called to me yet I could answer to only one. Whatever choice I made, it would consume me completely.

"Since I was the light, I repelled the darkness,

which feared me and crept away from me. Thus it will fear you, but be careful for it may creep around you unnoticed and secretly cloaked. Darkness is dangerous for it can cloak itself as false light, but it is murky and dull. You will know darkness in others for they will lack luminosity. Never betray yourself or your intuition, which is my voice within you. Listen to your inner turmoil, for it will awaken when darkness is near.

"My chariot made great noise as it rumbled through time. I saw all things yet to come. My golden carrier shook all beings to their core when I rode past, and those who weren't standing on solid footing fell. Those who were firm in my spirit rose in my heart.

"The sky has always been my friend. The sky held me and my dreams, and eventually carried me to my resting place. Father Sky reveals all things if one knows the language He speaks. I rode to the stars and they welcomed me, for things appeared as I arrived...this is how creation works. I am the illuminator and the one who restores all things. Look in my eyes, Dreamer, and see all things there.

"When I was last a little boy on earth, I rode the chariot when all were asleep. Had they known, my parents would have been afraid for me. Out of the sky it appeared, and rode into my home quietly to reclaim me. In the middle of the silent night, I stepped in. My old friend, the wind, blew and wiped my face, mind, and soul of all that clouded my memory. In the crisp night, the chariot of my life awakened me. Where it would take me, I did not know. My heart filled with love and off it took, led away by the horses chosen to lead it.

"We rode through many layers of the sky up to the highest level of Heaven, where the Divine was waiting for me. He was so happy to see me. Right before His feet the chariot stopped. Peace. I climbed out and was humble before Him. He greeted me with His eyes, His love, and His embrace.

"He told me how happy He was to be with me again. He told me I was chosen, and that I was mighty. And He told me I was the bearer of all truths. He opened His great book and read to me. I was the first name on the first page. He read the whole book to me. I was the last name on the last page. He told me all things began with me and all things ended with me.

"As He read the book and read my life, all things I remembered, for He had written all this upon my soul when I was created. He told me there would be pain but that I could endure it because of Him. I knew fear but it did not dwell in me for I saw the crown I would wear. It was made of the same gold as the chariot. It, too, would blind those who could not see and illuminate those who could.

"For this great glory, I would suffer. As the Divine read from His great book, He looked at me with a loving gaze. I could choose not to walk the path set before me, and that if I so desired, He would rewrite His great book. Yet I also knew that He knew better than I, and that His great wisdom went far beyond mine. In that moment, I knew all that He knew.

"Yielding completely to Him, He revealed Himself to me. We were no longer separate but one, part of the same soul, part of each other. I then had the power to choose, to create, to bestow, and to heal. To Him I owe all things.

"From that moment on I would never be apart from Him. He held me close, Father to Son. Tears fell. Wiped were they by His gentle hand. I was enveloped in His love, in His robe, and His armor. I did not want to leave but I had to claim my eternal place and to blaze a path for others to follow. I had to.

"As the quiet chariot waited for me, I stepped in.

Silently we rode back to where I began my journey, my boyhood home on earth. Yet the ending was the eternal beginning.

"I stepped out of the chariot when I saw my boyhood home. No one heard me. I lay awake all night, as I had been awakened, eternally. From that day forward, I saw the Divine. He was with me always, and remained with me. I walked through the rest of my life on earth with power, grace, and sustenance, all because of Him. I endured and overcame all because of Him. Finally, at the end of my life, I rode the chariot Home and took my place by His side.

"Now I have my own book. It is I who bring in the new time. For when I reign all time will cease to exist. My chariot and golden crown still serve me and will serve you if you follow me. Just as I had a choice, so do you. You may choose or deny at any moment the words I have written for your life."

# Chapter Three

~

## *The Beginning*

Deep in meditation, the Master spoke to the Dreamer. "In the beginning I manifested the mountains, the water, and the stars. All that is and ever was I created with love, peace, and harmony. Wait upon my word for it is true and swift. Justice is mine. All who challenge me will be defeated. Look up to the sky and you will see I am here with you, always.

"When I was a little boy, My Father, the Divine, told me, 'Son, you are too old for tears, yet too young for such sadness. Why is it that you cry?'

"My soul retained all the sadness it had ever felt, for I had grown weary of doing battle with the dark one, and I was filled with grief from all the tears the world had shed.

"The Divine understood and took me into His secret chamber, the place no one knew about. We were deep within the chamber but were surrounded by all the elements of the universe.

"My Father had also grown weary of battling the dark one, but said He would never give up. Eternal victory was the only destiny for us, He said. 'One must never give up, never!' He declared.

"He began to teach me things about the darkness, how it worked, how to protect myself from it and remain in the light. Darkness loved to seep into the light and disguised itself as false light."

The Master and His Father sat in the Divine sacred chamber for many hours. Together they meditated and had many visions of the future.

The Master said, "I exist in all dimensions, on all planes. I see and know all. All of life comes from me. I am the Source."

He promised to watch over man, His beloved brother, because His Father, the Divine, asked Him to. Man was alone and sad and needed a guardian, and so He came, but not for long. Man did not understand his purpose in the beginning... he still does not.

Still in the secret chamber, He read His Father's book of life, the book of all things. Only because His secret and innermost thoughts were pure was He allowed to read it. The Master read about other worlds and people His Father knew. The Divine wrote His book so that all who read it would have joy. The Master felt the book was alive because it was written with the word. His energy ran through His body, down His arm, and into His hand and into the book. The Master studied its pages to see what it would reveal to Him. He didn't know what the pages would say; He only knew how the book would end. The enemy would lose, as He always knew, but would put up a fierce fight.

"Always look for peace. Create it where it does not exist," He read aloud.

The Master knew He would need to teach His brothers and sisters this, but He also knew it would be a difficult lesson for them to learn. Contemplating what He had read in the Divine book, the Master walked deeper into the chamber, to a window, which revealed eternity. He stared out at all that was His Father's kingdom. Crystals were everywhere, especially the fields He was blessed to call His.

He chose one crystal and clutched His fist tightly around it, asking it to speak to Him. He loved these prisms of life and everything His Father created for Him. He was their inheritor and caretaker. Gazing into the crystal, the Master saw reflections of Himself and events to come. After a few moments, He gave thanks to the crystal for its wisdom and revelations, and gently returned it to its home.

\* \* \*

"Listen for Him, Dreamer, in the wind, feel Him in your dancing, hear Him in music, and look for Him in the moonlight, for He is there always. He speaks the truth, and is here to guide those who follow Him with an open heart and all who hear with an open soul."

The Dreamer ended her meditation and knew her life had been transformed by her vision. Eagerly she awaited her next vision.

# Chapter Four

~

## *He Said "Yes"*

The Master greeted the Dreamer, "Never fear, Dreamer, for I am with thee, always. I walk beside thee constantly. Know this to be true. The cycle of life is about to be complete. One step at a time. All things come to fruition, especially things planted long ago. The seeds are ripe, and the harvesting must begin.

"Dreamer, you see things most never see. All too often, most look beyond things that are meant to be seen. In your heart you know this to be true. Those who weep choose to. Those who rejoice took courage in me. I know the truth for this is my bounty and my bounty knows no end.

"Some have called me powerful, some have called me weak. Yet I am everything. I am the way and the word whispered in the night to all who have the courage to hear.

"The flight will be brief, the journey miraculous. The destination is illumination. I am the illuminator, the torchbearer, the one who lights the way. None can go before me. I show the way, the path to walk upon, for the power lies in gentleness and love.

"I have walked all paths before you, Dreamer. I know every wound that can be inflicted. My feet know every bruise and blister on every road walked. I know the weariness you feel, the exhaustion of your soul."

The Master held out His hands and made a rainbow over His head with blue crystals. The Dreamer took it all in as she sat in deep communion with the Master.

* * *

The Master continued, "I wanted things of beauty, and so I asked the Divine, and He created them for me through the word. The word is my dream and desire born out of love for things of beauty. The word, the beginning, is my wish and the Divine granted my wish by creating the universe.

"I asked for light and He gave me light. He created crystals, which hold all light, as well as the sun, moon, stars, water, rainbows, fire, and eyes for they, too, reflect the light of the eternal soul.

"I asked for trees, skies, and land, and all this He granted me. I asked for food, and instantly it was mine. All things live within me, yet I was once so lonely that the Divine created man. He breathed His spirit into him and I was happy. I watched my brother grow and learn, but he didn't know me at first. My brother filled my heart with joy and my world with laughter, and when I saw that man was lonely, too, the Divine created woman.

"Then man was no longer lonely, but he was led astray. He became blinded and could no longer hear the Divine. Once man could no longer hear the Divine, he was lost."

The Master was hurt because man and woman did not trust the Divine, and their betrayal wounded Him deeply. Because of this pain, He walked deep into His home to pray, meditate, and heal. Man and woman thought the Master grew silent, but He did not. He became deaf for a while because He dwelt in a womb that sheltered Him from pain, and He did not want to hear the sounds of the world for a time. All that He asked from His brother and sister was trust.

The Master continued, "Time past and I kept waiting for my brother to return Home. I kept hoping he would hear the Divine again, but lost hope the farther away he wandered from Home. I kept thinking, 'Surely in time he will return and then I can make myself known to him.' But he did not return. I watched the spread of evil and warfare on earth as time passed. The wailing and weeping wretched my soul. The cries were too loud for me to bear and so I chose to reveal myself.

"I asked the Divine if I could walk beside man. 'Surely if I walk beside him, my brother will know me, and hear the Divine once again.' To my plea, the Divine answered, 'Yes.'

"So that I might help my brother, I joined him on earth. I walked first as a little boy, then as a man. My Mother comforted me, my father guided me, and the Divine protected me. Always underneath His protection, I was safe. Some knew me, some did not, and others did not care and lived as if asleep. Dreamer, you know me, you hear me, and you listen to me. Always allow me to guide you, and I will never lead you astray.

"A long time ago, when I asked my Father about these things, He never thought man could turn against Him, for man was a part of Him. My enemy, the leader of the crafty, led man astray for his own plan. He hated me and wanted to take my place as king. My Father would never allow this, so the evil one hated me and all who love me. Yet I protect those who love me, those who are good and kind, humble and meek. Through me, they too, know all answers. What is mine will one day be theirs."

\* \* \*

The Master continued, "The Divine armed me

with mighty angels, great forces of strength and light who were powerful and fierce. Knowing all things, He also gave me might, towering luminosity, and courage beyond all understanding. My soldiers are fierce and stronger than my enemies. You are strong too, Dreamer, and are protected and full of light. You will blind the darkness with your brightness. Shine.

"Even with my army of angels, I had to walk many paths alone, but never forgot where I came from. Deep down I always knew I was not alone, yet lonely times and nights were many. My Mother feared for me but tried to hide it. She knew more than She revealed, yet Her eyes expressed what She could not. Her grace and sustenance still nourish me... the eternal Mother, divine holder of peace and prosperity.

"There is another yet to come. He will walk the path of peace and righteousness, as He comes for the last time, to defeat the enemy and to take with Him all who choose to go Home. Remember, in that moment I am with you. The beginning and the end. The word. Those who choose to go with Him will hear the Divine again and live in His kingdom.

\* \* \*

"Even now I watch over all of you and my soul aches for those in pain. I comfort all even though some cannot tell I am with them. I always am there for them, in the night, in the silence, in the eyes of an angel, I am there. I know all secrets, all wounds, and all nightmares long before you have them.

"It is not just to suffer, yet it is noble to endure. I did not ask you to suffer in my name, the evil one did. Yet out of your love for me, you endure and transform your suffering into light.

"All things begin with me and end with me. I am the judge, the king, and the Master. This I earned with my love, peace, compassion, and courage. All who suffer in my name will know my peace and have a place in my royal court, the palace of all palaces, and the kingdom of all kingdoms. This I asked of the Divine and He said, 'Yes.'

\*   \*   \*

"There will come a time when there will be an uprising of all light workers, all who have been training in silence. They will arm themselves with the word, ask the Divine for His help, and He will say, 'Yes.'

"They will rise up and take their divine place as peacekeepers of the earth. They will then call my name, and I will come. They will ask me for my divine peace, power, prosperity, and love, and I will say, 'Yes.'"

# Chapter Five

~

# *The Light of the Stars*

The Dreamer knelt in Heaven waiting for the Master, waiting for His word. Finally she saw Him coming.

"Master, you have arrived," she said.

"Dreamer," He said, "I am always here. It is you who have arrived."

He raised His arms and enveloped her with His robe. In the blink of an eye, the Dreamer felt what He felt and knew what He knew. Then she saw the stars. The Master began to tell the Dreamer tales about the stars.

He pointed to His favorite one and said, "That is where I was born," as it shimmered and blinked. "You see Dreamer," He continued, "it remembers me. My Father chose this star because it was pure, radiant, and full of love. All things need to be loved. Everywhere I go, everywhere I have been remembers me eternally."

The Dreamer looked at the star and then at the Master and saw that the star also lived in His eyes. He remembered every place He had ever been. Everything He has ever seen, felt, and touched lives within Him.

"Master, where was I born?" she asked.

He pointed to the same star.

She asked, "How can that be? I am not as pure

as you are, Master. I want to be, but I know I have made mistakes in my life."

"You were born there, Dreamer, because you wanted to be. Your deep desire to be with me is the reason you were born there."

She was overcome with awe and gratitude, and asked, "Master, why must I live on earth? Why can't I be here with you all the time?"

He looked deeply at her for a long time, "Because I asked you to live in the world so that others will know I am always with them."

The Dreamer was humbled and silent.

"You are always here with me in spirit, Dreamer, yet at times you are not aware of it. Never doubt you are always here with me."

Out of His pocket, the Master took a small clear beautiful crystal and gave it to her. She held the crystal in her hand and looked deeply into it. The crystal held the light of the star within it, and as she looked at it a while longer, she could see the reflection of her eyes, shining with the light of the star.

"Keep this with you always, Dreamer, and remember to look at it when you feel you are away from me. It will remind you that you are here with me and that I am with you, always."

She held the crystal in her hands and lowered her head to touch her cupped hands, and then thanked Him for His gift. She knew that as she was a part of Him, the small crystal was part of her. The Master sat down beside her, still enveloping her with His robe and His spirit and together watched the stars that live in Heaven.

# Chapter Six

~

# *The King of Kings and His Throne*

"Dreamer, when I was a boy I would sit at the Divine's feet waiting to become just like Him," the Master said. "His throne was grand, built around His mighty being. It was encrusted with jewels of every color, living and breathing within pure gold. I could always see things inside the precious gems... stories of eternity. I saw that all things lived within His throne.

"At His feet, I was so small yet completely loved and safe. When He had work to do, He would rise from His throne and sometimes walk away. During these times I would crawl up and sit in His place, hoping one day to reign with Him, beside Him. When I sat in His throne, nothing was beyond my sight. Even as a child, sitting in His throne, if I thought of something, I created it."

\* \* \*

As a boy, the Master sat upon His Father's lap. Together they sat upon His throne and watched eternity. The Master did not want to reign alone, nor did He want to take His Father's place for He wanted them to reign side by side.

In time, a throne was especially built for the Master. Hundreds of angels poured their love into their creation for the Master. They came from all corners of the universe, all reaches of Heaven, to build for Him the holy chair. Each angel brought something special, something miraculous from his or her domain. One brought gold, another brought rubies, and another brought the holy velvet. As it began to take form, the Master noticed that His throne was an exact replica of His Father's. The Master watched and was proud, and when they finished they knelt before Him in a circle.

As He watched a vine of ivy, it wrapped around everyone and grew up the bottom and side of the throne, giving its blessing. The ivy had grown by the time the throne was ready for Him. With great excitement and anticipation, He eased himself upon the throne. His Father was proud for He knew He had suffered to sit there. And that is where He remained...seated in eternal purity, reigning by the side of His Eternal Father.

As the Master sat and watched, He could see the universe and every galaxy within it. Every thought He had materialized, every feeling became real and visible. Sitting upon His holy throne, the Master knew He had great power and great responsibility, and the most difficult duty of being eternally pure.

# Chapter Seven

~

# A Blade of Grass

The Master held a blade of grass in His right hand and swirled it around, smiling.

"This is the beginning of all things," He said to the Dreamer. "From this blade springs life. It receives light and gives breath, just as you do."

He walked a few steps away from the Dreamer towards a small pond and picked up a small stone. The stone was solid in hues of black, brown, and gray. It was nothing special nor out of the ordinary, but as the Master held it, it glimmered and glowed and became purple.

He walked back to the Dreamer and sat down in front of her. He beamed at her as she met His gaze and looked at the stone in wonder. The Master smiled.

"Dreamer, all things are like this stone," He said. "Look at it. At first it looks lifeless, without breath. It looks dark, empty, and cold. Yet in my hand it becomes light, free, alive. In my hand it is awakened, it breathes and lives. You are like this stone, Dreamer."

As she looked deeply into the stone, the Dreamer saw herself. She was dancing in an ecstatic trance to music her ears could not hear. Her eyes were brilliant with light. All levels of the Dreamer were in harmony.

She looked at the stone in amazement, yet she was not surprised for she knew the Master could do all things. The Dreamer looked at the Master and He smiled at her.

"All the great mysteries are revealed by things we walk on or don't see," He said. "If one were to look deeply at all things, one would find the same answer. You know the truth, Dreamer."

The Master reached behind Him and brought forth an oil vase made of clay. It, too, was nothing out of the ordinary. Somehow she knew this piece of holy pottery. He held it in His hands for quite some time, and studied the Dreamer carefully and lovingly.

He then said, "I have kept this all this time."

The Dreamer smiled at the Master. As she looked at the bottle, she could see through it. The inside of the glowing bottle was a porthole to the beyond. The Dreamer could see light, and far in the distance she saw angels. Some were walking and meditating, others were flying, some were dancing and laughing, and all created music with their movement. This radiance was pure light in one dimension, and in another it was holy oil, scented from Heaven.

The Dreamer reached through the bottle with her hand and felt the oil as her hand went through the clay. She looked up at the Master and laughed in wonderment. He joined the Dreamer in her joy. The oil transformed her and changed the energy in her body as she was filled with light.

The Dreamer flashed back in time to when the Master walked the earth. She saw Him in a humble house. It was dark, cold, and damp, yet it was safe because He was there. There was one white candle lit, glowing in a clay holder. It was resting on a wooden table the Master and the Dreamer sat around. The Master spoke. The Dreamer grew afraid for she sensed what was to come, and reached for the bottle filled with the precious oil perched high on a wooden shelf.

The Master and the Dreamer were suddenly alone. She looked at Him and knelt before Him. With her hands and with her tears, she washed and wiped His feet. Sobbing, she bent over and held her hands over her hair on His holy feet. With compassion He looked at the Dreamer and smiled, filling her with His peace. Looking at Him through swollen eyes, the Dreamer felt His peace fill and envelop her. The Master and the Dreamer were again in Heaven, looking at the bottle, seeing another dimension.

"I was there, Dreamer," the Master said.

She withdrew her hand from the bottle and saw that it glimmered. The Dreamer caressed her face and felt it come alive. She rested her fingers lightly on her third eye and felt something forming in her right hand... a white crystal took form in the center of her palm. It blinded her for a moment with its brilliance.

When her vision appeared again, the Master and the Dreamer were surrounded by hundreds of angels, all smiling at them. The Dreamer felt safe and excited. They all held white, lit candles and formed a circle around the Master and the Dreamer.

The Dreamer felt something move again in her hand, and realized that the crystal had become a lit candle, and was clear white, brilliant, and prismatic. She held it in delight and smiled at the Master and the angels. She was filled with unconditional love.

As the Dreamer looked carefully around the Master's feet, she saw the small blade of grass planted in Heaven's soil. The plain rock lay beside it and the Master watered it with His holy oil. The grass swayed beneath His hand. Beside it the Dreamer planted her candle and laid her head at the Master's feet content and filled with gratitude.

# Chapter Eight

~

# *A Handful of Sand*

The Dreamer was floating in the Master's blue sky and a dove appeared. It gave her an olive branch that it had been carrying in its mouth. She held it with delight.

An angel appeared and gave her a white flower, a lily branch... Gabriel. He took the Dreamer by the hand and led her to another beautiful place, and began to draw images with his olive branch in the sand that lay beneath their feet. As he drew, the Dreamer could see he had been drawing the live mural for centuries. It lived in another dimension.

Each piece of his mural was delicate yet resonated with energy. He held the Dreamer's hand and lifted her a bit so that her feet wouldn't crush any image. Holding his hand, she floated above the magnificent map of humanity. All parts of the world were drawn... all countries, all places, and all events. In a way, he was the Divine's illustrator.

As the Dreamer looked at each part of the sandy canvas, she felt all the emotions that were present. The longer she gazed, the more began to happen. She saw wars, famine, peace, prosperity, death, birth, and life. She wondered why all of this was drawn in sand, by an olive branch, held by the Archangel?

He looked at the Dreamer for a long moment and

then handed her his olive branch. She could feel it pulsate in her hand. Holding it, she had to draw with it, for it would not rest until it had given birth to life. She felt unworthy to hold it, but Gabriel instructed her. Still holding his hand, she knelt beside him, her knees not disturbing the tiny crystals.

She was so nervous. She didn't know what to draw so she prayed. Then she knew... she would draw her life. As she drew, she knew the olive branch was creating and leading her hand to where it wanted her to follow. It had an energy that was more powerful than her hand. It was charged and divinely electric.

As the Dreamer's hand followed the olive branch, her life appeared before her. All the pain and hardships, and all the joy and love appeared, yet as she drew she could only feel the love. The painful moments were drawn vaguely, indicated and suggested, while the joyous times were drawn radiantly and elaborately. It was as if only the good remained in life, while the pain disappeared.

The Dreamer looked up at Gabriel when she had finished, asking what he thought. Still holding her hand like a father, he knelt down beside her to look at her work. He smiled and was proud.

"Well done," he said.

The Dreamer returned his olive branch and he looked more carefully at her creation... a line here, a shadow there, a softer edge, a muted foreground. As he adjusted and corrected her drawing, he adjusted and corrected her life path. They sat for a moment and studied the tapestry of sand. She was amazed that all people were connected to each other and were all part of the same mural. One soul could not exist without the other.

"All lines on this tapestry run into one another," he said. "Each feeds the next like water. Water runs into itself. Tears are shed because of separateness.

Unity brings joy.

"If I spread my hand across the tapestry, in one moment I could destroy it, it is that fragile. Yet the Divine does not allow that. He upholds and protects the weak. So instead, my hand makes this strong, built to withstand eternity."

As the Dreamer looked across the horizon of sand, she saw tiny lights flicker, as if it were a city. In one moment, all the lights on this mighty mural ignited. She smiled and took joy in its splendor. When she looked at Gabriel, his olive branch was lit, a flame and torch of the Divine. It was burning, yet its leaves and flowers were not destroyed. He smiled at her and lowered his head to touch the branch to his forehead. Gabriel then offered it to the Dreamer. She, too, lowered her head and received the branch upon her forehead. All at once, she saw great light fill her head and the rest of her body. It was as if an explosion of light ignited her third eye. She closed her eyes to savor the moment.

Gabriel touched the Dreamer's forehead again with the branch. She felt stronger and filled with even more light. She fell asleep for quite some time and when she awoke, she was still in the Divine's blue sky, kept company by the dove, and in her hands she held the olive branch, the lily, and a handful of sand.

# Chapter Nine

~

## *The Flame That Burns All Things*

The Dreamer was humble before the flame, a pillar reaching high in the sky beyond her eyes. She bowed her forehead into it. The flame burned through her third eye, cleansing and igniting it. She could now see things she could not before. As her vision opened, so did the universe before her.

She saw the great chariot again, ridden by the Master. He rode towards her and stopped off in the distance, as it was she who needed to complete the journey, not Him. She walked through the flame but was not burned. Each step she took covered miles as she floated towards the chariot. As she approached, she saw the grand spokes of the golden wheels.

The Master stood up and welcomed the Dreamer, holding the reins in His hand. She stepped into the chariot upon His invitation. The seats were covered with maroon velvet and were soft and plush. The ornate decorations of gold mesmerized her. Sitting beside the Master in His golden chariot, she felt completely safe and loved. All her worries disappeared. Finally, she was going Home.

The Master smiled at the Dreamer and turned to steer the chariot Heavenward. She closed her eyes for a moment and gave thanks. She began to feel the wind gently toss her hair. The air was sweet and she could hear the music of Heaven faintly playing. When she opened her eyes, she saw the angels flying beside them... all luminous. All loved the Master. All who flew by them touched the Dreamer's hand and kissed her forehead. There were millions of angels, some off in the distance, but all were very powerful in love and light.

The Master and the Dreamer rode through many heavens, and many skies of different colors. Each sky had a different feeling, a different energy, yet all were magnificent. The Dreamer saw the saints, the martyrs, and the meek... all were happy, all were saved; some faces were familiar to her.

As they soared higher, the Master's robe caressed her face. She saw His life, what He went through, and what He had suffered. She felt His sorrow, His pain, and His regret, yet he could not be buried. The earth and man could not hold Him. Her soul wanted to sob but she felt His joy, His love, His eternity, and His peace. She felt the reign of His mighty kingdom and knew He held that as tightly as he held the reins of His chariot.

When they arrived at the final resting place, the most glorious part of Heaven, the Master gave the command for the chariot to stop. He stood up and stepped out of the golden carriage and held out His hand to the Dreamer. She stood up, took His hand, and stepped out. There was no ground but her foot stood upon a solid foundation. White, opalescent clouds surrounded them and glorious music played without end.

The Master told the Dreamer, "Anything you want, Dreamer, is here. You only have to imagine it."

# Chapter Ten

~

# *The Mirror*

The Master and the Dreamer were in Heaven sitting on a large, smooth rock. They were surrounded by peace, tranquility, and love, and the horizon was illuminated pink, imbued by the light.

"Look over there, Dreamer, and you will see all things," He said to her.

She looked to where He was pointing and saw only the light.

"Come, let us have a walking meditation," He said.

They walked through the clouds and the clouds whispered to them in the wind. The Dreamer understood their message and felt embraced and loved by them. The Master loved the clouds, the wind, and the light. He loved His home.

As they walked further along the path of Heaven, they saw clouds of heavenly lavender, which radiated the same peace, yet enveloped them differently. In the purple light, the Dreamer heard music her soul recognized, even though she had never heard it before. She wanted to linger in the purple light, yet the Master led her forward into a blue she could not describe. The angelic blue, indescribable in its peace, wrapped them in its heavenly aura and the Divine music soothed her soul.

The Master began to meditate in His perfect silence, while the Dreamer watched Him for a moment, devoted to His breath. As He inhaled, she inhaled and filled her body and soul with His breath. Then, she closed her eyes and joined Him in meditation filling her soul with divinity. With each breath she drew closer to Him and the glorious blue light. She became the music, the wind, the clouds, and part of the light. The Dreamer met the Master in vision and she saw Him holding a mirror.

As He held the mirror to her eyes He said, "The mirror sees everything."

The Dreamer looked at her reflection and saw that her once dark brown eyes had become clear blue green and were full of light. Her hair looked like white light and glowed around her ancient yet new face. She was mesmerized. She continued looking at the mirror into another dimension. Eager to see everything her illuminated eyes could see, she focused her attention on the mirror. Her entire life was visible in the mirror, things she thought were secret as well as the things that were known to others. The Master then turned the mirror slightly and she saw another part of her being. In the Master's hand, the mirror could reveal anything.

He smiled. "The mirror sees things even you cannot, Dreamer."

The Dreamer saw her higher self, who watched over her at all times. She couldn't see much of what was to come in her life, but saw that it was all very beautiful.

"This is my favorite place," He said.

"I love it, too, Master. Thank you for bringing me here," she said.

"You are welcome Dreamer, but I merely showed you a piece of yourself, a piece you are entitled to know. Always be mindful of that part of yourself. Carry it with you always," He said.

# Chapter Eleven

~

## *The Jewel in the Forest*

"Tell them about the jewel in the forest."

The Dreamer looked past the Master following His pointing arm. Behind Him was a deep, lush forest and off in the distance glistened a bright stone. It was luminous and its light called the Dreamer close to it. She could hear her footsteps gently touching the forest floor as she walked to be near it. All that she could see was the stone as each step drew her nearer. Finally, she was before it and as she gazed deeply into it, was hypnotized by its beauty. She looked back and could see the Divine watching her and was comforted.

Suddenly, the Dreamer was pulled within the stone and filled with its light and brilliance, and with joy, peace, and eternity. She felt its walls with her hands yet she was not its prisoner. Gold light filled the air and beautiful music played. Within the walls of the stone chamber, children ran and played and sang. All were happy there. The Dreamer looked at her hands and realized she had not changed form, but was different and full of light.

Through the walls of the stone, she could see the Divine calling her back to Him. Though she did not want to leave the home of the beautiful stone, no call was greater than His, so she ran quickly to Him.

"How did you like the jewel in the forest?" asked the Divine.

"I loved it," the Dreamer replied.

"Good, because I want you to have it," He said.

"What did I do to deserve it?" she asked.

"You gave me a gift, Dreamer. You came to me when I called you. You chose me over your desire. You came to me because you love me. You came to me because you heard the word and obeyed it."

The Dreamer was filled with unspeakable gratitude.

He held the stone in His right hand... the jewel of the forest. "This once belonged to the Master, my Son," the Divine said. "The word dwells within it. Keep it safe and cherish it. I will see to it that no other possesses it."

He put the stone in a small pouch and tied it tightly. He put it around her neck so that it would be with her always.

"Remember, Dreamer, the word and the jewel are one," He said.

# Chapter Twelve

~

## *The Stone*

"The stone and I are one. The stone is solid, impenetrable, and firm," the Master said to the Dreamer as He caressed the sand around a small rock.

The Dreamer put her hand in the sand to feel what He felt. Gracefully, He lifted the stone and held it in the palm of His left hand. He raised His hand to the sky and looked lovingly at the stone. As she watched Him, she noticed that the gray stone had miraculously become a ruby. Light bounced within it and from it, but only as long as it was within His hand.

"This stone and I are one," said the Master. "It rests in the ground... damp, dormant, alone. Yet in my hand, the hand of love, it becomes a glorious and precious piece, incapable of being anything less than magnificent.

"All walk by the plain stone, yet all want the precious ruby. They do not want to appreciate it, only to own it. There is one simple law of love to obey Dreamer, and that is to love the stone before one knows it is a ruby."

With His right hand He took the Dreamer's left and held her palm heavenward. In it He placed the gem and stared deeply into it. She felt it burn her hand, yet she was not in pain. She was amazed that it remained a ruby in her hand, for she felt that without His touch it would not shine, yet His gaze was upon it and that illuminated the small stone in her hand.

The Master guided the Dreamer to hold the ruby. As she closed her hand around the stone, she felt it pulse. Its energy traveled up her arm straight into her soul igniting a light and fire within her. The red heat of the ruby forced her to bolt straight up and she looked at Him for answers.

"Some may not truly know you, Dreamer, but do not despair," said the Master. "I know you just as I know this stone. I have disguised those who belong to me to protect them, just as I have protected this ruby. I have the power to cloak what is mine, and the power to illuminate what belongs to me. This stone is the same to me whether it is dark and covered in mud, or if it is a brilliant ruby, blinding all who look at it, because I know its true form. I know its true identity, just as I know yours. Do not fret if others walk by you thinking you are no more than this stone in its muddy form, for I know you are the ruby, more precious than anything else."

Tears seeped out of the Dreamer's eyes as she looked at the Master. Holding her hand in His, she lowered her forehead to touch His hands.

"Thank you, Master," she said.

The Dreamer used the fringe of His robe to wipe her eyes, and as her vision cleared, she saw dazzling rubies appear on His holy garment. She looked at Him and He smiled. So many secrets were held in His eyes, mysteries He earned the answers to long ago. He was the way, the path, and the light for the true believers. All she had to do was follow Him.

"I want you to keep the stone, and keep it in this pouch," He said as He showed the Dreamer a beautiful satchel with a long cord. "Wear it at all times, as it will remind you that I am with you always."

He helped her put the ruby in the satchel and then placed it around her neck. Immediately, she felt the weight of the stone call her forward.

"Dreamer, things that are unseen hold the greatest treasures. Know this to be true." He put His hand in the sand again and picked up another stone, dull in color and soft to the touch. As He did before, He gazed deeply into it and moments later it was ablaze with His light.

"Come, Dreamer, let us walk," He said.

She took His hand and walked with Him along the beach that stretched out before them. Along the way they stopped to pick up other stones that had been discarded by those who could not see within them. As the Dreamer looked behind them, she could see millions of glistening gems where there were once lifeless stones.

All things came to life in His presence. All things awakened as He passed by, and all that were asleep were awakened.

Walking beside Him and holding His hand, she breathed the air of His kingdom that filled her soul with eternity.

"Master," she said, "I will never let go of you."

"Good, Dreamer. I will never let go of you either. Even if one day you cannot feel my hand, know that it is eternally wrapped around yours. Know that I am with you, always."

"I know, Master," she said.

He filled her with His love and peace. He would always be with her just as He had promised, and she would always be with Him just as she had vowed. She learned that the ruby and He were one because both were precious, indestructible, and filled with the Divine light.

"One day, Dreamer, you will walk by stones and they will ignite beneath your feet," He said, "but you must be ready for this, for they will burn if you are not prepared. Prepare by believing in my word. Believe in the law of love and all that you pass by will be illuminated with the light of the Divine."

# Chapter Thirteen

~

## *The Thorn Bush*

The Dreamer saw the vine of the thorn bush that was to become the Master's crown and wondered if it knew beforehand what its purpose was. The vine was green and alive, full of life's juices, and looked like it could cause no pain, even if one held it close in their hands. The thorn bush was part of every soul... and the spirit of the thorn bush lives.

Heavy hands chose this vine. The Dreamer watched it leave its host bush, its family, and felt its trauma at being broken off. She realized that upon His head, it was not meant to hurt Him, although those who placed it wished it would. The vine, sealed in place upon His head as a crown, was anchored there for its own journey home. Somehow the Master knew this and was not angry at the vine that caused Him pain. Though its thorns pierced Him deeply, He would not shake the crown from His head.

In the Dreamer's vision, the crown was covered with His blood, yet it made the vine more alive. It did not die upon His head, but found its life within His blood.

The Dreamer saw them place the crown upon His head and she saw them crucify Him. No words could speak of her grief. She was shattered.

The Dreamer also saw Him walk away from the

cross they tried to secure Him to. He walked with joy, defeating death's iron door and gliding through eternity. As He walked, the Dreamer saw the crown in His hand as He held it lightly, it was emblazoned by the light and surrounded by its glory. He walked in a pasture of light and nothing but love followed Him. Blades of illuminated grass grew toward Him eager for His touch. Carefully, He placed the crown among its own, returning it to the family it was cut away from. Miraculously, the crown uncoiled itself to join the others. The Master smiled as He looked upon the reunited greens.

# Chapter Fourteen

~

## Crown of Thorns, Crown of Diamonds

The Dreamer saw the Master walking toward her in her meditation, in a white linen garment. It was filled with Heaven's light and air. She bowed before Him and He looked at her with great love and light. He held out a box to her and slowly opened it, revealing His crown. Spellbound by the sight of it, the Dreamer watched the Master gently lift it out of its box and place it on His head. As He did, the crown of thorns became a crown of diamonds.

He whispered, "What makes you bleed eventually makes you shine."

The Dreamer held His hand and kissed it and as she did, all of her wounds were healed at once, His radiance restoring her completely. As she looked at the crown, the diamonds were uncountable, and she could not stare at them for long as they were blinding. The Master selected a diamond from His crown and held it out to her.

He said, "Swallow this and it will make you whole."

Humbly, she took the diamond from Him and put it in her mouth. Slowly, it began to dissolve and its taste was of Heaven. She felt the diamond clear her throat and all obstructions within her being. As it settled in her stomach, the Dreamer felt its heat, and in a moment euphoria set in. She looked at the Master and understood what He was telling her.

"All wounds must be open for a moment, and must hurt for a while, but I have the power to heal them, and remove the pain forever. Remember this always."

"Master, I will remember," she replied.

Her hands and skin glowed because of His radiance and her clothes transformed into robes of His secret colors.

The Master said, "Many people have been looking for this crown and will continue to search in vain. Where they look they will not find it. They do not understand that to find my crown, they must look within their hearts. Dreamer, you found it because you kept your gaze upon me. Never lose sight of me for I will protect, sustain, and love you. No one can follow you here, but if they know the truth, they will find their own way here.

"I have hidden many secrets within the earth and all secrets lead here. Only those who are humble and kind will find them. One cannot get lost if one follows the path of the true secrets and only I can reveal them. Absolute surrender delivers everlasting grace, the key that unlocks all doors and reveals all secrets. The only way to find that key is to worship me and I will honor you with my love and salvation."

The Master revealed a gold chain He had been holding in His hand.

"This is my chain of life. Each soul who follows me is a link. You see that it is unending, but soon I must finish it."

The Dreamer knew the chain had links beyond her vision.

She asked, "Master, which one am I?"

He pointed to the one He held in His hands. "You are this one, Dreamer."

He moved His hands further back in the chain and said, "And you are this one, and this one, and this one," moving His hands back in time as He moved them to the beginning of the chain.

By His teaching, the Dreamer could see that His children were links on His chain of life and that He cherished them all. They were important links at the beginning of His chain as well as toward the end. The Dreamer could see He wanted to finish His chain soon.

Knowing her mind He said, "Dreamer, soon I will wear this chain in my kingdom and all who are a link on it will be with me always."

To be with Him eternally in His kingdom, with everyone she had ever loved who had passed over, is what she always wanted. She would always surrender to His wisdom and return home holding His secrets in her heart. She thanked Him for His grace and knew that whatever wound she suffered in her life, He would heal it and transform it into a link on His chain of life and carry her Home.

# Chapter Fifteen

~

## *Think of Me, Think of Me*

"Think of me when you are sad, Dreamer. Know that I have been there, too. Walk with me and I will lead you to unseen pastures. Only those who walk with me will see this valley as it was prepared for those who hold my hand. Only I know the way," said the Master.

The Dreamer could see flowers, grass, mountains, clouds, and blue skies. They were in the perfect place. The air was clean, and breathing it healed her, as she could taste it with her being. They walked toward the castle, way up in the mountains, and as they strolled, He stopped and knelt down to pick a flower. He held it to His nose and inhaled its fragrance. Then He gave it to the Dreamer to do the same, and she was hypnotized by its fragrance.

The Master looked at her and said, "Let us return it to where it belongs."

He guided her to place the flower back at its home, and she laid it on the grass. The Master held His hand over the flower and its roots grew back. It looked happier for having been picked and chosen.

The Dreamer knew the Master was showing her that even though she sometimes felt cut off from her life, from her home, from her loved ones, she was always in His hands. Sometimes being picked up in

His hands hurt, but only for a moment. When He cut away the Dreamer's stems to hold her in His hands, He only cut off what she no longer needed. It dawned on her that she must detach from everything if she was to rest in His hands forever.

She looked at the Master and smiled, knowing she had fully understood His teaching. They walked some more, and suddenly the castle in the clouds seemed much closer.

The Master said, "When you finish your life, then we will enter the castle. Until then, this is as far as you can go."

The Dreamer was content to be with Him in the beautiful meadow, filled with the peace that only He could create. They sat in the tall cool grass and let it caress them in the Divine gentle wind. She closed her eyes and lost herself in His light, and knew one day she would be able to stay beside the Master forever. At last, she would be Home.

# Chapter Sixteen

~

# *The Sacred Cottage*

The Dreamer knelt at the Master's feet. He smiled at her and draped the sleeve of His robe over her head, enveloping her with His being. She felt completely safe, and was lost in His radiance. Every storm within her was calmed because she was once again with Him.

Taking her by the hand, he led her to His kingdom. As they journeyed, stars flew by them and layers of deep energy blanketed them. As she surrendered, she saw everything He wanted to reveal to her. Then they stopped in the place most radiant. He stood facing her, pouring His light and love into the Dreamer. Never before had she known such complete peace.

"Come Dreamer, follow me," He said.

He led her by the hand to a small cottage, opened the door and motioned for her to go before Him. It was as if the house had been carved into a cave, or a tree, or a mountain. Though it was of Heaven, it held something of the earth within it. Crystals hung from the low ceiling. Blinding light filtered through its windows. Red pillows lay on the floor. Soon, the Dreamer realized this was where the Master meditated, prayed, and wrote.

She felt humbled to be there, and asked the

Master with her eyes if she could touch the sacred pieces of His holy world. He nodded in response. The Dreamer touched the scrolls, tablets, and loose ancient papers, and though she couldn't read the ageless text, she understood their meaning, and felt their writings deep within her soul. The paper held an energy that traveled through her fingers to the depths of her soul. She gazed into the crystals, hypnotized by their beauty and clarity. As each one danced in the wind, she saw different angels fly through their prisms. The Dreamer was in a place of pure magic and mystery.

The Master motioned for her to sit and meditate as she felt the red velvet cushions. The Dreamer joined the Master in spirit, prayer, and breath. As they faced the light, they breathed deeply and she felt His peace fill her soul. She could think of nothing else but the joy He filled her spirit with. So complete was this peace that the Dreamer's worries disappeared. They meditated for what seemed like hours and when the Dreamer sensed their joint prayer was complete, she opened her eyes to look at the Master.

He opened His eyes as if returning from another dimension and smiled at her.

"Dreamer, you are always welcome here. All of my children, and all who love me are always welcome here."

"Thank you, Master, thank you," she said as she humbly kissed His hand with tears filling her eyes.

# Chapter Seventeen

~

## *The Potter*

The Dreamer was watching the Master at His potter's wheel. He was so focused on the clay before Him that she was hypnotized by watching His creation in progress.

"Welcome Dreamer," He said. "I am working on another vase. The others I created are beautiful yet imperfect. I cannot rest until I create what I see in my mind's eye."

He motioned with His head for her to look at His pottery. The Dreamer walked into a vast room filled with hundreds of thousands of pieces made by the Master. They were placed on shelves that reached to a ceiling beyond what her eyes could see. Their beauty was astonishing and light lived within each piece. Each different color held a vibration, an energy, and a feeling. Each piece seemed to have a soul. She couldn't imagine what was imperfect about them, but realized the Master had the soul of an artist, not satisfied until He manifested His vision. The Dreamer walked back to Him and watched.

The Master worked at His wheel, seeing something the Dreamer could not. And though He seemed frustrated, His face was filled with joy and luminosity. He infused each piece of pottery with His light through His eyes and hands.

"Join me, Dreamer," He said.

"Master, I don't know what to do," she said.

"You must only begin," He said, handing her a small piece of clay.

"What do I make?" she asked.

The Dreamer centered herself and thought for a moment. Then the Master wrote upon her soul.

"I will make a box," she said.

"Very good, Dreamer," He said.

With great care she began to form a small box. The Dreamer could feel a piece of her soul pour into the clay as she crafted the small container. Her clay seemed dull and not as extraordinary as the Master's, and she looked at Him for help. With His gaze, He lit the box with a dazzling inner brilliance.

"Thank you, Master," she gasped.

She worked on the lid of the box and carved a small star in the center of it. She added details to the box and lid so that when it was finished it looked as if pearls and diamonds lived within it.

"Well done, Dreamer. Let us complete it," He said as He carried it gently to His kiln.

As He opened the door of the kiln, she saw other pieces inside, perhaps made by His other students. She couldn't wait to see how her box would come out. He smiled at her as He shut the door.

"Patience, Dreamer," He said as they waited.

Time passed. Then He opened the door and let her look inside the kiln. All of the pieces glistened. Her box had grown considerably from its former small size, and the Dreamer was amazed.

"Master, it is so beautiful. What should I do with it?" she asked.

"Hold my treasure in it," He said. "My gifts will never end."

Tears welled up in the Dreamer's eyes. The Master took the Dreamer's box from the kiln and handed it to her. The Dreamer graciously accepted it from His hands.

"Thank you, Master. I will always cherish your gifts, and hold them in this box forever," she vowed.

"Open it," He said.

Inside was an enormous ruby lit from within. She held it in her hand and heard glorious music as she held it to her ear. As it sang to her, the Dreamer lost herself in its bliss.

"My gift to you, Dreamer," said the Master.

"Master, I am beyond words," said the Dreamer, filled with gratitude.

The Dreamer wanted to hold the ruby forever. Knowing this, the Master gave her a golden chain He made and wrapped the ruby in a gold sheath so she could wear it always. Holding it in her hand and feeling it around her neck made her feel close to the Master.

The Dreamer put the lid back on her box, and knew when she opened it again there would be another gift from the Master. She gave thanks to Him, grateful for His gifts of grace and peace.

# Chapter Eighteen

~

## *Footsteps in the Sand*

In deep meditation, the Dreamer was walking on a beautiful beach as the sun was heating and illuminating her path. Ahead of her, she could see the Master as His light shone around Him and infused the beach with His spirit. As she looked at the sand, there before her were His footprints, which she knelt to touch with her hands. She felt His power fill her and began to walk in His steps. The Dreamer felt each step with the sole of each foot, and forced herself to walk slowly, to feel each grain of sand as she followed Him. No matter how slowly she walked, He was always in front of her, never walking farther away.

As she continued, He stopped walking to wave her on. Her steps hurried as she began to run to Him, still within His footprints. The closer she got to Him, the deeper were His steps in the sand. Finally, she reached Him and fell at His feet out of breath.

The ocean wind whipped through her hair and she could taste the salt water. Yet the only thing she could think of was Him, how He led the way, how He suffered for us, how He waited for her. He put His hand on her head and touched the crown of her head. Immediately, the Dreamer's breath was restored and she heard the chanting of angels.

"Know who you are, Dreamer, and where you

belong," He said.

He smiled at her and filled her with the light of His sun. He held up His hand and calmed the wind, and as He did, the waves subsided as well. All obeyed His command. The Dreamer remained at His side until the sunset, and then they continued walking on His glorious beach.

# Chapter Nineteen

~

## *The Hallway of Souls*

Deep in meditation, the Dreamer walked through Heaven... eternal dawn. The clouds were sweet and carried Heaven's music. Her footsteps made no sound and her garments flowed silently as she awaited the Master. Finally, the clouds parted and she saw His holy home. His palace glistened, brilliant in its purity, and was alive with His love and peace. Somehow she recognized it, as she must have been there before but had no conscious memory of it.

As she stepped closer she could see the doorway, a beautiful golden-ivory arch. As she walked beneath it she felt His peace envelop her. She continued to walk down a long corridor, passing secrets of the universe with every step. A great power lived in this hallway and the Dreamer knew it must have been the hallway of souls where all depart and where all return.

In the distance, she heard a soft knocking and looked to see what the sound was. Although there had been no door when she walked through the hallway, she saw one beneath the golden archway when she looked back. Someone was knocking on the door yet there was no answer. She could see the person knocking had done many evil things in his life, for all of his evil deeds followed him to the doorstep. He could not walk through the door.

Then she heard the Master's voice, "He is not repentant for what he has done. If he were sorry for the sins he committed, then he could walk through the door."

\* \* \*

The evil man finally gave up knocking and began to walk away as the spirit of his evil deeds enveloped him. The Dreamer felt sorry for him yet knew that he had designed his own fate long ago.

"Come forth, Dreamer," said the Master.

She continued walking down the great hallway of souls. It was a serene place, a place of reunions and restoration, and a place where all souls traveled to heal. Then the Dreamer was led to a great fire burning upon a marble column. She felt deeply drawn to it and stared intently into its fire.

"Your eyes do not burn even when they gaze into the mighty heat," the Master said.

She lost all sense of herself and saw only the fire and heard only the Master's voice. At that moment His hand reached out to her. As the Dreamer held it, she was drawn to His side. They were suddenly in a secret chamber... blue velvet curtains draped the walls and the room was filled with a deep, rich light.

"I watch all souls leave and I watch all of them return," said the Master. "As they leave I talk to them, and when they return I talk to them. No soul walks through this hallway without seeing me, and I record it all in my book. And when it is all recorded, I will give my book to the Divine to keep in His holy library. My volume will be the last."

As He spoke to her she could see a handful of souls coming Home, and one or two departing. He recorded everything: every moment, each thought, and every journey of each soul. The Dreamer was fascinated at how much He wrote for each passing soul.

"I love them all," He said.

He watched each soul come Home with great love and relief, and watched each one leave with deep love and concern. He trusted the Divine completely yet worried for the little ones returning to earth, so harsh a place at times. He knew some would struggle terribly to return Home, and to these He gave an extra part of His soul. He gave His love, light, protection, and peace to all. If all the souls lived on earth with a piece of Him inside, He knew they would one day return safely Home.

He smiled at the Dreamer and said, "I love them all."

"I know, Master. They love you too, as do I," said the Dreamer.

Standing beside the Master in His holy chamber, the Master and the Dreamer watched the souls float through the great hallway, embarking on new missions or completing ones they had been assigned. The Master loved each one deeply. All who walked through this hall loved Him just as deeply. None could enter who didn't love Him. All who were sorry for things they had done, or who loved Him deeply were allowed to stay forever.

# Chapter Twenty

~

# *The Dove*

Deep in meditation, deep within Heaven, the Dreamer followed a pale blue bird flying in front of her, flying effortlessly through the clouds. It dawned on her this was no ordinary bird, but was the bird... the dove of the Holy Spirit. She could feel its spirit as she flew, sensed what it knew, and felt in her soul the bird's truth and knowledge. The Dreamer felt the wind caress her face, whispering a language she didn't consciously know, yet understood.

Following the dove, she flew forward to an opening in the sky. They hovered at a high altitude above the earth, upheld by some sort of force field. The Dreamer continued to follow the dove, as her soul was tucked beneath the wing of the dove. Immediately she felt pain as she gazed at the buildings that interrupted the beauty of the planet.

Suddenly, way below them, the Dreamer saw a brilliant blaze of light in the middle of what looked like a desert. The dove spotted this light and flew quickly to that spot because it saw the Master.

The bird had flown to the side of the Master and rested on His shoulder. Its mission was to announce His true identity, heralding His appearance on earth once again. The Master greeted the bird, recognizing His friend. The bird was loyal to Him and only Him.

Though the Master walked the earth, He dwelt in Heaven.

The Dreamer's vision continued as she watched years pass. The dove always went before the Master and never left His side. The dove foresaw all things and prepared the way before Him. The dove protected Him from all that it could, yet could not prevent what was written. Even at the end of the Master's mission on earth, the dove flew by His side and cried for the pain He suffered. Yet the dove also joined the Master's flight Home and the eternal celebration.

The Dreamer knew the Master and the dove would always be inseparable and learned that whenever she saw the bird in flight, whether in vision or with her physical eyes, that the Master was near.

# Chapter Twenty One

~

# *The Obedient Sword*

Deep in vision, the Dreamer saw the Master's outstretched hands nailed to the cross. Her focus turned to the nail driven into the center of the beam of the cross. The pain on the Master's face was indescribable. It looked as if the cross had taken the life out of Him, yet through the Divine, it had given Him and all creation, eternal life.

*   *   *

"The relic must be found," said the Master.

Staring at the nail in the cross, the Dreamer looked at Him, unsure if the Master meant for her to find a piece of the cross or the nail itself.

"The relic must be found," He said again.

She dropped to her knees and asked, "Am I the one to find it, Master?"

"Yes, Dreamer, but I will guide your way."

The Master showered her with His healing rain, as the Dreamer eased her head back, purified and cleansed on all levels. Then, she was suddenly in a vast desert with the wind whipping the sand up in a silent storm. For miles she could see nothing but desert and felt overwhelmed.

"Master," she cried, "what do I do? Help me, please," she begged.

"Walk toward the light," the Master said.

She didn't know which direction to walk, as everywhere she looked there was desert.

"Master, please help me. Show me the way," she pleaded.

A path of light was seared into the desert sand. Wearily, she followed the illuminated path. Knowing not where she was going, she trusted the Master to lead the way. Willing each foot in front of the other, she pressed onward. The sand and the sun burned her face, but the Dreamer persevered. The sands of time marked her face and etched its story upon her canvas.

At last she could see a small forest of trees on the horizon, so brilliantly green, their lushness beckoned her to hurry. The Dreamer almost ran to the treasure of trees waiting for her beyond the desert. As she neared, she saw a small pond of clear, holy water, and immediately slipped in. Underwater, she was free, cool, and weightless.

As she surfaced for air, she looked around and saw that the forest had grown to fill the desert. A large oak tree beckoned to the Dreamer, so she got out of the water and sat at the foot of the great shade bearer. Its leaves enveloped her, and she felt life pulsing through the veins of its limbs.

"Here is the relic," said the voice of the tree.

She looked towards the direction of the voice and saw an enormous, magnificent sword stuck into a large boulder.

"Draw the sword and cut off my arm," said the voice of the tree.

"With what strength? I cannot draw that sword nor can I remove a limb from such a beautiful tree," she pleaded.

"Do as I say!" the voice commanded.

The Dreamer walked over to the huge rock and

observed the sword more closely. Encrusted in its handle were rubies, sapphires, pearls, and an ancient inscribed shield. The handle was made for bigger hands but she knew she had to draw this sword and do as the voice told her. She climbed upon the rock and deeply centered herself. She connected with the center of the great boulder while holding the sword in both of her hands. Breathing deeply, and ultimately without much physical effort, the Dreamer felt the stone release the sword. She was awed by the sword and felt its magnificent power.

"Now, cut off my limb!" the voice commanded.

She didn't want to harm anything so beautiful but knew she had to obey the command. Hesitantly, she walked to the tree and found the limb nearest her reach, telepathically asking its permission to be cut off. In one motion, she cut the limb off from its trunk. Blood rushed out of the tree, and the Dreamer watched it pour to the ground. When she looked upon the earth, she saw a nail deeply embedded in a small piece of wood.

"You have found it!"

Suddenly, the Dreamer was before the Master once again, and took the relic in her hand and presented it to Him. She knew she was not meant to keep the relic, but to feel it, experience it, and tell others about it. She held it in her hand and fell asleep for hours. The relic transformed the Dreamer and healed her, revealing sacred visions to her. It held miraculous powers because it held drops of His blood and all of His pain.

"Enough, Dreamer," the gentle Master said.

She gave thanks to the Master for this miraculous experience, and glorified Him.

"Now, Dreamer, take your sword and lift up the branch you cut down."

She did as she was told and the branch

miraculously became part of the tree again.

"Use the sword wisely," cautioned the Master.

"I will Master. And every night I will return it to its resting place."

"Well done, Dreamer, well done," said the Master.

# Chapter Twenty Two

~

## *The One Who Suffered*

The Master said, "It is I who suffered greatly for man, yet I survived time and conquered death. It is I who bear the torch of eternity and hold it high for others to see. And it is I who will carry it into the darkness to light the way for those who wish to leave the dark.

"I burn with the Divine's light. On fire with His flame will I blaze and remain forever. The light conquered death and all who dwell within it, and as the light conquered death, I conquered evil.

"My crown turned into diamonds, transforming thorns into stars. All who wear it will know the way and be saved. All who wear it will never walk in darkness again. If one can stand the pain of the thorn, one will know the glory of eternity.

"My hands have healed and no longer bear the holes chiseled by man. Yet it is I who will carve out man's destiny. My side no longer bears the scar of the lance, yet I have turned the lance into my staff and hold it in my right hand. I will use it to judge those who scorned me, and love and protect those who love me.

"We must have compassion for one another, even those we do not love, for they need it the most. If one can be saved, then it is worth loving all. Many will disappoint, yet one may be uplifted, and it is that one we must help. If there is a chance to save our brother we must try. We will not be here much longer and when we leave it will be forever. When we walk through the doors to eternity we will not return. And for this reason we must gather as many as we can, for those left behind will remain forever lost.

"It is up to you to find them, Dreamer. Seek them out, tell them your stories, and show them the way. If they do not take it, you have done your work. And if only one takes the way, we will have been victorious.

"All preparations are being laid for my return. I will return but only for a brief time. I will gather those who are mine, and return Home with them. If they are not ready, they cannot come, and if they are ready, they will not return to the world. Know this and be prepared.

"In the blink of an eye I will come and even quicker will I leave. I carry all the secrets of the universe and all the hearts of those I love. You must cherish me for I cherish you and nurture you like an infant. No one will guard my flock the way I will. You must be careful. You must not become lost for there will be many who will try to mislead you. Do not follow them for they will come in my name, but you will know in your soul that they do not know me.

"They will be jealous and deceitful. Disregard them and stay on course for you light the way for others to return Home to me. I will always keep you safe. Never fear for I am never far from you. Even though you may not see me, I am with you. Look for me without your eyes and you will always see me.

"Wear my robe and follow me. You will never need another garment. Walk in my footsteps and you will never become lost. Share the truth with others and they will know that I have sent you.

"Leave your worries and sorrows with me. With

my feet they will be crushed, for I am the one who suffered and the one who conquered death. Because I conquered death, I am the one who lives the victorious, eternal life. And because my life is eternal, all who dwell in me and with me live forever. Tell this to all who will listen."

# Chapter Twenty Three

~

## *The Holy Robe*

The Dreamer kneeled at the Master's feet. The top of her head touched His garment and she could feel beads of oil at the fringe of His robe. As the oil touched her head, she felt a warm bath of energy caress her wounds, both of the flesh and of the heart. Her hands were moist from the oil of His garment. She touched them to her face to cleanse and purify herself. As the oil purified her, it also healed her spirit like a flame of fire burning through her soul. She looked towards the sky and saw the stars blanketing Heaven.

The Master asked, "What are you looking for, Dreamer?"

"You, Master," she replied.

"You have found me," He said.

Lost in His eyes, she was lost in His peace. His eyes blinded her, as she could see nothing but Him. Transfixed by His gaze, the Dreamer was no longer separate from Him, and realized she had never been separate from the Divine.

The heavens raced behind the Master, stars flew by, and clouds whispered around them. It was as if they were traveling through time. She felt transformed by the heavens moving through them. He was everything... the stars, the sky, the moon, and the earth, the radiant sun, the wind, the rain, and the vast oceans. He manifested everything and resided in every creation. All of this, she saw in His eyes.

As she looked at her hands, she noticed that her arm looked like water, as if the ocean lived within her skin. The Dreamer's feet seemed filled with earth, and fire seemed to live in her belly. The wind moved through her hair and the clouds caressed her face. Stars visited the palms of her hands, and she could feel the Master's great white light illuminate her eyes.

Loving Him transformed her into a small reflection of Him. All the elements He had created now lived in her. Seeing His magnificence and being in His presence made her realize she had always belonged to Him. That He revealed great secrets to her was a gift she humbly cherished. The Dreamer knew He was alive in all things, and in all places. The Dreamer realized that He was with her always, even when she was sure He was not.

"Go and tell what you have seen, Dreamer, for they need to know I am here," pleaded the Master.

"Master, I will tell them everything," promised the Dreamer.

# Chapter Twenty Four

~

## *The Illuminated Cloth*

Deep in meditation, the Dreamer found herself beneath an illuminated cloth. Silver and gold light filled the material that draped over her head reflecting the light from the eternal flame. She reached up over her head to feel the holy fabric, and as she did, her hands were covered with a rose-scented oil that she then touched to her face.

A hand lifted the cloth and gently revealed to the Dreamer where she was. The light that filled the air was all consuming and peace giving. Immediately, she bowed her head before the angels, who each held a piece of the same fabric over their heads. The angels smiled at the Dreamer as if they held a secret, motioning to her to hold the cloth with both of her hands while it still rested over her head. As she did this, the Dreamer's hands began to pulse and glow. She smiled in amazement and looked at the angels for guidance.

The angels bowed their heads and lit a large white candle in the center of a triangle they had formed. As soon as it was lit, the candle became an enormous flame. All bowed their heads into it. The Dreamer closed her eyes and as she did the same, her third eye erupted with visions. She saw the Master walking toward her, holding the same cloth that lay over her head across His two arms. It was blood stained in certain places and tears rolled from His eyes as He walked closer.

Still in a vision, the Dreamer dropped to her knees, crushed by the pain she saw in His eyes. She couldn't believe what they had done to Him. Tears burned her eyes. The Dreamer felt her soul burn with the agony He must have felt so long ago.

When He stood before her, the Dreamer cried, "Master, how could they have done this to you?"

He put His hands on the back of her head, filling her with His spirit. Under the cloth, the Dreamer saw visions of what He went through. She felt His pain and sorrows, His loneliness and fear, yet she also felt His union with the Divine, a union no one could destroy. For this and for His suffering, He was greatly rewarded with the kingdom only His followers could see. He removed the cloth from her head, folded it, and placed it in His sacred chest filled with many treasures.

He sat beside her and said, "Dreamer, the cloth placed upon your head is a blessing that will remain with you for all time. The cloth is mine to keep and guard, for its power is sacred, miraculous, and powerful. Trust me."

"Master, I trust you with my life, with my soul, and with my world. Yours is the kingdom I seek. Your treasures are those most precious to me. All that I want is to be by your side, at your feet, touching the hem of your robe," she said.

Resting His hand on her head the Master said, "Then you have found what you have been seeking, sweet Dreamer, and this is where you will remain."

# Chapter Twenty Five

~

# *The Shroud*

The Dreamer saw the Master walking toward her on the water, carrying something in His hands. His light was blinding and it filled her with joy and peace. As He got closer the Dreamer knelt before Him. She could see that He held a long, sheer, white luminescent cloth. He draped it over her head and when He did, a vision appeared of Him wrapped in the cloth: His eyes were closed, His hands were crossed over His chest, and His wounds were cleansed. He smelled of precious oils and His skin shone with Heaven's light.

The Dreamer's heart was shattered, as she wept by His side. She couldn't see through her own tears, her grief was inconsolable. Her soul wanted to escape her body to be free of the pain. At that moment, she felt a hand on her shoulder and she was instantly filled with peace and love. It was the hand of the Master, yet when she looked at Him He looked slightly different.

"Dreamer," He said.

"Master," she replied.

She let the tears flow from her. She closed her eyes to see more of her vision. She saw the body that lay quiet, covered in the holy cloth, and it, too, carried the aromas of Heaven and burned with His light.

Again the Dreamer looked at the Master and He instructed, "Cover my body and I will be with you always."

Still in vision, she knew He meant for her to cover His body, gently and lovingly, and that in doing so He would be with her eternally. The Dreamer also felt the excruciating pain of losing the Master when He lived on earth.

She cried, "Master, please don't leave me!"

"I will never leave you, Dreamer," she heard Him say.

She grieved as she covered His sacred body for the last time, and prayed and kissed the Master's hands and feet one last time. She had to let Him go so that He could live eternally.

The Master's light was even brighter than before. He seemed to grow in power as He released His body to the Divine. The Dreamer then saw a glow emanating from His heart where His hands had been crossed. It grew in brightness until she could see nothing but the light, and then all the light swirled into the Master and filled Him completely. His eyes shone with a piercing intensity. Instantly the body was gone, and only the cloth remained.

"Gather it in your arms and leave this place at once," said the Master. "Others will look for you and will want to steal the cloth, but you must guard it with your life. Others will want it for the power it holds."

Stunned by His words, the Dreamer quickly gathered the cloth. She folded it carefully and hid it within her robe. She knelt in prayer and thanked the Master for His blessing. She asked to be made worthy of such a gift and for His help and protection.

"Go, Dreamer, now!" He commanded.

Still in vision, she ran to her home, bolted the door behind her, and gathered what little she had, knowing she had to leave at once.

"Go to my Mother, She will know what to do," the Master told her.

"I will go to Her," the Dreamer replied, "but Master you must help me."

Covering her head and most of her face, the Dreamer ran out the back door to the Mother's house, where She was waiting for her and knew they both had to disappear. In the back of Her house were two horses and all of Her belongings were strapped to them.

"The Divine has provided for us. We must leave now. We will be safe," the Mother said.

With all of their belongings, the Mother, the Dreamer, and their two guardian horses rode for miles. The Master walked beside them the entire way, lighting their path. The cloth was safely protected within the Dreamer's robe, and as they rode, she felt its heart beat throbbing against her chest. At one point the Dreamer could barely breathe.

"What is it, Dreamer?" the Mother asked.

"I am carrying His cloth and it carries His heart. I must see to it that it always remains protected and safe," the Dreamer replied.

The Mother looked at her with love and admiration. She knew she was carrying a piece of Her Son with her and felt comforted by this.

The night they rode seemed endless, yet He continued to lead the way. They stopped to rest finally by a small cave, carved into a mountain by the water. Fresh food awaited them in abundance. Beautiful clothing was laid out for them and they knew they were safe.

"Wait here until I tell you to leave," cautioned the Master.

They waited for what seemed like years, yet they were happy and safe for He was with them.

Then one morning He said, "It is time to leave."

Once again He led the way. The Mother and the Dreamer returned to Her home and lived the rest of their days there. The Master never left them and when it was time for the Dreamer to leave her body, He told her what to do with the cloth to keep it safe and hidden. She followed His words and followed Him Home.

The Master held the Dreamer by the hand to carry her across the water he had once walked on and took her Home. The Mother was already there, sitting beside the Divine, waiting for the Dreamer. She knew one day another would carry the cloth Home and lay it at His feet.

The Dreamer knelt in prayer and bowed before them, filled with ecstatic and eternal joy. She was Home at last, lost in her vision.

# Chapter Twenty Six

~

## *The Sandals*

Kneeling at the Master's feet, the Dreamer recognized the Master's shoes and couldn't take her eyes off them. She held His feet in her hands and stared at the leather straps through tears that filled her eyes. Were these the ones she had made for Him, she wondered? She knew those shoes... they were worn and soft, and covered with a thin dust of earth. She knew He no longer needed them, yet why was He showing them to her, she wondered? He loosened the tied straps and handed the sandals to her.

"Walk in them, Dreamer, and return them to me," He said.

She humbly accepted the holy shoes... holy because He had worn them. She fell asleep at His feet and when she awoke she was alone, yet she was wearing His shoes. Silently she rose and eased to her feet. Her feet felt alive, as they never had before. Energy surged up her body, and in a bolt, she was filled with His light.

"Walk, Dreamer," she heard His voice say.

The shoes led her forward on a path she was not confident to follow. With His spirit, she walked for miles through hidden pathways, up mountains, along the ocean. All ground was made sacred beneath His sandals, even if one of His children was wearing them.

The more she walked the newer the sandals became, as if their journey restored them because He had once walked in them.

Then she heard the Master's voice. "My sandals served me well until I no longer needed them. They crawled the distance with me and wore out, yet in their service they earned the reward to be with me eternally.

"You made them for me long ago with love and devotion. Because they were made with such love, they sustained me and helped me walk when I could not go on. As you wear them now, your love and devotion to me restores the shoes to their infant state.

"The reason I came long ago was to show others how to walk. That my shoes carry on in my name and spirit is proof that I have succeeded, for they know the way Home and will lead many there."

The Dreamer realized the Master was telling her He needed us to go on in His footsteps, so that His shoes would always be clean and new, as wearing them renewed His steps.

The Master's sandals continued to pull the Dreamer forward. In them she walked through His entire life and felt every moment as if it was her own, overcome by joy, love, peace, grief, pain, and tears. Finally, the journey ended.

She looked at her feet and saw that the sandals sparkled. She dropped to her knees and gave thanks to the Master. She was grateful that she had been given the gift of walking in His shoes. She bowed to the ground, praying to the Master. When she lifted her head and opened her eyes, she was at the peak of a very high and holy mountain. The sun was slowly setting and the air was crisp and sweet. Then out of Heaven, walked the Master.

The Dreamer couldn't take her eyes from Him. In His hands He held a large clear bowl filled with water.

The water glowed as He set it down by her feet. He took the sandals from her feet and eased them into the bowl of healing water. At once, she felt all pain and sadness leave her. As she looked at the sandals in the bowl, they disintegrated into liquid gold. Then the Master held the bowl to His lips and took a small sip.

"Drink this," He told the Dreamer as He held the bowl to her lips.

As she drank the liquid gold, it filled her body with strength and sustenance. She could see things she could not before, and the only emotion she felt was love.

"Come, Dreamer, let us walk," He said as He took her by the hand.

Behind them they left the bowl sitting upon the mountaintop. The farther away they walked, the more it filled with liquid gold, waiting to quench the thirst of all who would make it to the mountain top, walking in His shoes.

# Chapter Twenty Seven

~

## *Many Lives, One Spirit*

The Dreamer was in Heaven, humble before the Master. She watched Him walk through several bodies, as if His spirit walked through many lifetimes. Who were they, she dared to ask herself. It didn't matter for they were all the same being. The same soul walked through many bodies and many lifetimes, and stood before the Dreamer. He looked the same as He always did, and His peace filled her and His gaze hypnotized her.

"Do not seek others, for I am here," said the Master. "Do not run from who you are for I will always find you. And do not give up faith or hope for that is the link that binds you to me."

"Master," she said, "it is you I have always sought. Your words are the only ones I have longed to hear. False prophets speak false words, but your truth always sings in my soul."

"Dreamer, you do not believe all the time," the Master said. "You must watch and guard your faith. Do not leave an opening for fear to spread its dark cloud within your spirit. Listen to me and I will transmute any darkness."

"Master, forgive me for my fear and doubt. Why I have held so dearly to it I do not know, but I place it at your feet," the Dreamer cried as she released everything to Him.

"Well done, Dreamer," said the Master, "for I know what to do with your fear and doubt."

The Master waved His hand over the fear she had left at His feet, which looked like a pile of dark ash. Beneath His hand, His holy flame ignited her fears and raised them as a ball of light to the Master's eyes. He carefully studied this ball of fire as if He were looking deep within her soul. The Dreamer knew the Master saw all things. Then, with His holy breath He blew on the fire and it dissipated into white smoke.

"Let it go, Dreamer," He said.

She closed her eyes and breathed deeply, releasing from her core all that she had held onto that was not full of light.

"Dreamer, let it go," He said once more.

As she let the Master's words soak into her soul, she let go of all the fear, all the pain, all the sadness, and all the tears. She was with Him, and all that remained was His spirit. The Dreamer opened her eyes and exhaled as she watched the white smoke travel to Heaven. She was free.

# Chapter Twenty Eight

~

## *Feel My Wound*

"Take my hand, feel my wound, open my heart and the blood of the world will pour out. Touch my heart and you will feel pain, yet leave your hand upon it a while longer and you will feel only my peace and love," said the Master.

The Dreamer touched the Master's heart and dropped to her knees before Him. It was as He said. At first she felt the pain of the world, including her own sorrows, living within His heart. The agony overwhelmed the Dreamer.

"Leave your hand there, Dreamer," He encouraged.

As the Dreamer left her hand upon the divine heart, a calm came over her. All sorrow left her. The Dreamer did not know how He held so much sorrow yet so much love and peace at the same time. He transformed everything into light and joy.

The Dreamer bowed her head and closed her eyes, bathed in warm light and immersed in His spirit. The Master had poured His heart upon her and the rest of the world. The sorrows of the world poured forth freely from Him, and He seemed free of a burden He gladly bore. He watched the sorrows leave Him as birds from a nest, yet the sorrows were transformed into great joys and brilliant light by His hand and heart.

At last, she understood what He meant when He said, "Open my heart and the blood of the world will pour out."

# Chapter Twenty Nine

~

## *Baptism*

In meditation, the Dreamer was humble before the Master. Never before had she seen so many tears in His eyes. He took her hands in His and held her eyes with His. She felt His profound sadness fill her spirit. Never before had she seen the Master so sad. The Dreamer was afraid for His grief. He held His glistening crown of thorns upon His head and stood before her in a radiant white robe.

"It is too late," He said.

The Dreamer asked, "For what, Master?"

"For the few to listen, as those who are stubborn will never hear, and those who hear will be too afraid to speak. Listen to me for I know and speak the truth. What you will hear from others will be lies, but be careful, for their deceit will sound as truth. In your heart, you will know what is the truth and what is false. Never question what I reveal to you in your soul, for there is where I reside. If you choose to ignore me, you will never know the truth or my peace. Always listen, even when your heart and soul are weary, for my words will always protect you and guide you," He cautioned.

The Dreamer held onto His hands, her tears blending with His as their tears fell upon their joined hands. The puddle they formed at their feet turned to aqua blue and she felt healed as the warm water of tears began to swell up in her eyes.

The Master put His hand on her head and lowered the Dreamer beneath the water's surface. In His tears He baptized her and cleansed her impurities. She felt the darkness and pain leave her and watched them drift away in the Master's healing pool of tears. Gently He lifted her above the water's surface and looked at her deeply, knowing all pain and sorrow had left her.

"Arise and take your position, Dreamer," He told her.

As she did, the Dreamer gazed upon the horizon where millions of angels were filled with His light and love.

"Dreamer, go and join them."

# Chapter Thirty

~

## *Ruby Tears*

The Dreamer was in Heaven standing beneath a shower of rubies, the ruby showers that were His tears. Through the ruby tears the Dreamer saw Him walk toward her.

"Dreamer, listen."

She heard the soft rhythm of the dropping rubies, and as they fell upon her she felt peaceful.

The Master said, "Look, Dreamer," as He waved His arm across His grand horizon.

As she looked across the horizon she saw the ruby showers take form in His kingdom. They floated into shapes of rivers, mountains, sacred caves, and beautiful homes. Everything that was magnificent and holy, the ruby showers became. The Dreamer looked at the Master in amazement.

"Dreamer, all of the ruby showers are souls who have cried out for me. I have never forgotten them, and thus, they became my tears. Each soul that has ever cried out for me remains with me forever. They do not cry alone, for I am with them always. Look around you and see the glory their tears become in my house. Their tears are precious, just as the ruby."

The Master held out His hands to catch a few ruby drops.

"My hands can never become full," He said.

"There is always room for another ruby drop, one more soul. All one has to do is cry out for me, either in joy or in pain, and I will hear their cry and catch them. My hands will never tire of holding any of my loved ones."

As the Master held His hands out, a large ruby cluster formed in His palms. It glowed from within. The Dreamer could see it took a lot of His strength to hold it.

"Dreamer, I want you to keep this to remember me," the Master said as he handed her the miraculous gem.

"Master, I could never forget you," she said as she gathered all her strength to hold the precious ruby.

"I know you will never forget me, but others will. This is for them. You must share it with them so they know I am here, and care for their tears as I would a sacred garden. You must tell them this and show them the ruby, for they will need to see that their tears have arrived at my feet. You must do this for me."

"Yes, Master, I will," she said.

"Look deeply into the heart of the gem and you will see my life, you will see my tears and pain, and you will see my heart," the Master said.

The Dreamer gazed into the center of the ruby with all of her being. Her soul leapt into the heart of the ruby. There were millions of rubies, and all were filled with joy. She saw rivers of silver and gold watering pearl and opal flowers. Buildings were made of clear blue stones, and light emanated from all elements. Sadness did not exist within the ruby heart of the Master.

"Listen, Dreamer," said the Master.

She heard chimes and beautiful notes of music. How happy she was to hear it and join in with her voice and spirit.

"Remember me, Dreamer," the Master said, "to those who will forget, who have already forgotten, or who are already lost. I am here and all of their tears reach me. I will never forget them or their tears, as they are the most precious gifts to me, my ruby tears."

# Chapter Thirty One

~

## *The Ruby Chair*

The Dreamer was humble before the Divine, the Master, and the Mother. They led the Dreamer to a ruby chair and helped her sit upon it. It enveloped her, making her feel embraced.

The Master said to the Dreamer, "I will read you a story."

Her eyes, ears, and entire being were transfixed upon Him.

"Once, when I was a little boy, on a very special night, my Mother read to me from the book of life. She read my life and knew what would happen to me. This helped prepare her, yet it devastated her as well. I was too young to be frightened at the time, but something deep within my soul was stirred and uneasy. I knew I could not escape what was written for me in the book of life."

"I remember that evening," the Mother said. "I was terrified yet at peace, for I knew all would work out under the Divine plan. I understood very little but trusted the Divine completely in guiding our way."

The Divine said, "I have written everything, and have taken great care to prepare and plan everything. Every life is a thread in my great tapestry, which I cannot finish if it is missing one thread. It is the same with my book of life. It cannot be complete if one name is missing, if one page is torn out. All names must be written in it and read aloud at the appropriate time. All lives have been planned accordingly and they must follow my word for I am the great storyteller. All who come to me know my book and have followed what was written for them.

"All who sit on the ruby chair are allowed to hear my stories," said the Divine. "It is the chair I sit on when I write my stories, and where the Master listened to His story. Many things happen in this ruby chair, things that would seem impossible to those who cannot accept the miraculous."

"Father, why am I allowed to sit in this holy chair? What have I done to deserve such an honor?" the Dreamer asked.

"Because you believe in the impossible," the Divine replied. "It is easy for you to see us and hear us, because you want to. Your heart desires what it has found, and thus you have been granted your wish. Wishes are granted to all who truly believe and live with a pure heart."

The Dreamer was stunned. Her hands were hot from the energy of the chair and the magnificent presence of the Divine, the Master, and the Mother. She felt the chair form itself to her body, and felt it sink into her soul. There was a great silence throughout the universe. Stillness.

Then each one read a page of the Dreamer's life. Some of what was read had already passed and there was great pain in the reading for the Dreamer. Yet great joy was ahead for her as she eagerly hung on every word they read thereafter. There would be laughter and joy ahead for her that she was supposed to share with as many people as possible. Because she had known great pain, she would be able to understand the suffering of others. Compassion. The Dreamer had to trust them to guide her every step, reading from the book of life.

"Sleep now," the Divine said as they closed the book and formed a protective circle around the Dreamer.

She leaned her head back against the ruby chair and closed her eyes, filled with gratitude. For a brief moment, she saw the great book but could not read anything. She released her soul to them and her body to the ruby chair. The Dreamer exhaled into it and felt the ruby fill her spirit with its incandescent heat. She fell into a deep sleep, knowing she would have to do everything she could to share the teaching with others to help ease their suffering.

# Chapter Thirty Two

~

# *The Awakening*

The Dreamer wandered through the rainforest looking for her soul. It beckoned her deeper and deeper into its heart, and as it called, she answered. Enveloped within the canopy of its denseness, she sat and listened. Years passed, but to her, it was only a moment. She knew she was there to hear the voice of the Divine, and slowly she began to hear Him.

"You have been called to do great work," He said. "Courage for it will take all your strength and time, yet know that I am with you always."

The words fell upon her like rain.

"I have chosen you to lead people to me. For this, you will know great hardship and joy beyond your understanding. You must trust me for I know what you do not."

As the Dreamer listened, she couldn't imagine how she would help so many, yet she trusted Him. She believed He could do what she could not, so she sat and prayed.

Again, He spoke. "There are plans I have set out, which have taken centuries to materialize. After you, there will be many. By your courage and simplicity, you provide the path for others to walk upon. Your footsteps are light, yet they will leave deep imprints."

The Divine gave her the gift of story and vision to

light the way Home for many. She held the gift tight to her bosom, keeping it safe in her heart.

He said to her, "Guard this gift with your life, and it will give you your life."

The Dreamer buried her gifts deep within her heart. She vowed to protect the secret and sacred knowledge with her life, and share what she could in her stories. At that moment, she was awakened. Enlightenment.

# Chapter Thirty Three

~

## *The Tree*

The seed was planted long ago. The Master watered it with His tears and it grew to be a great tree. All who dwelt beneath this great tree were fed and saved, sheltered, and disguised from danger. All who lived beside her were cast in her shadow. All who walked away from her perished and were lost.

An acorn fell from this tree and sprouted another. Soon there was a forest, thick with light. The Master walked through this forest one day and sat at the foot of this great tree. The sky was blanketed with branches and leaves. He sat back against the mighty trunk and felt His back become part of the tree's skin. What was once hard became soft, and the tree cushioned the Master with her mighty limbs.

The forest floor was soft and smooth, and the cool earth radiated heat. The Master was alone yet He was one with all. As He leaned against the tree, He closed His eyes and rested His hands upon His bent knees. He breathed in the cool air, the sweet dew of the forest. It filled His lungs and entire body. As He tilted His head back, He became one with the great tree, the tree that would one day carry Him Home.

The Master felt everything the tree felt. The tree had known many fears, much pain, great isolation, and profound loneliness. Yet she was tall and mighty, strong and powerful. She withstood all things. She overcame all darkness. Her limbs rose above the Master, and through her the Master was carried to heights He could not see alone. He looked at the horizon of the entire sky. His eyes could see the universe because His feet stood upon the tree's canopy. The Master was not afraid. The tree would not drop Him. He felt the tree's branches move to carry Him, for that was the law.

The tree swayed in the wind and the Master heard its call. He danced with it, moved by its gentle breeze. His hair blew, changed color, and became translucent. He looked at the branches that held Him and they, too, glowed.

The Master's writing tablet then appeared. As He held and caressed it, He opened it to the page He had written on last, and gently placed His hand upon it. The word appeared beneath His hand. Whatever He felt, thought, and created appeared on the page. Gently and easily the words appeared from another dimension, first lightly and then powerfully.

He wrote about the tree. He wrote about how the tree had carried Him, healed Him, transported and uplifted Him.

As the Master sat perched upon her mighty branches, the pages of His book began to turn themselves, urging Him to complete the tree's part of the story... the word. The Master's tablet was anxious to finish, anxious for Him to know its ending. This was just one story, yet it was the story. When the Master turned to the last page, the word had already been written. The word went before Him and He followed with His soul.

The last page held a small branch pressed into the leaf. Its aroma overwhelmed the Master for He knew it well. The branch lifted off the page leaving its imprint upon it. It floated up to reach the level of the

Master's eyes and it lingered there. Then like a bird, it flew off into the distance, into the beautiful pink, luminous horizon. He knew it was going Home.

The Master watched it until He could see it no more. Then He closed His eyes to follow it the rest of the way. Finally it rested, but only at the foot of the Divine.

He picked it up gently in His mighty hand and placed it in a large bowl of water beside His throne. The small branch disappeared and the water was ignited. The Divine put His hand in the bowl and it caught fire yet didn't burn Him. His hand became translucent and His eyes lit up with His own fire. He looked at the Master as if He knew.

As He kept His eyes closed, the Master felt His back become hot, fiery, and heavy. He could feel the power of the one who knows filling His tablet with His pages. It took all His strength to hold His book steady. The Master's arms began to ache yet they remained strong. His spine began to burn yet it remained erect. His feet tingled and were scorched yet they could not move. In His complete adoration, the Master became like Him. The one who knows knew His soul, and made Him a mirror of the Divine.

The Master placed His writing tablet at the feet of the Divine and He gazed upon it lovingly. A small blaze erupted from it, yet it was not destroyed. As He looked within His body, His spirit was aflame. The tower of strength that lit all things ignited the fire in His soul.

# Chapter Thirty Four

~

# *Floating Flowers*

The Dreamer welcomed the rain upon her head for it was good and healing. She held out her hands to catch the raindrops and the sun came out and basked her in its warmth. She greeted her old friend and closed her eyes to truly see Him. At once she was dry and surrounded by flowers in their fullest bloom. As she walked along, she came to a river and was greeted by a large flower, a rose. It floated towards her and caressed the riverbed. Slowly and gently it invited her within as it floated back and forth in the pure water. The Dreamer stepped in and the bottom of her robe was wet, but she didn't mind, for the rose was warm. She lay back and relaxed deep within its petals. She trusted the rose to take her where it would.

The Dreamer and the rose floated upstream, somehow traveling against the easy current. In the distance the Dreamer could see a beautiful castle perched upon a magnificent hill. Fields of grass and flowers blanketed the hill the castle sat upon. Closer and closer they floated towards this magnificent home. It was held so high that she wasn't sure when or how they would reach it, but decided to trust that they would.

The rose began to float faster towards their

destination, and within an instant, they were before the great doors. The rose stopped and gently floated before the doors. The Dreamer looked up in awe at what was before her.

She stood up within the rose and touched her hand to one door. Slowly it opened. She stepped out of the rose and onto the ground before the doors. She looked around her and saw nothing but beauty. She caught her breath and stepped inside. She carried a drop or two of water, but they disappeared on the blue marble floor. There was no one around as the Dreamer walked down the long, magnificent corridor. She could see in the distance another set of great doors protecting the true, inner chamber of this great house.

She walked, but made no sound. She knew she was walking upon holy ground. Before she reached the doors, both opened and she could see a fire burning at the center of a round marble temple. The small bonfire burned within a circular marble structure, and she knew she was looking at the eternal flame. As she got closer, she could see gold and precious stones left around the fire as offerings and knew others had been here before her. She knew she was supposed to leave here what was most precious to her. The Dreamer knelt before the fire and prayed for the Divine to show her what she should leave.

He said to her, "Leave me your tears."

The Dreamer poured her eyes out and let her tears fall upon the flames of His fire. As they fell into the flames, each one sparked and crackled. She smiled as she watched them evaporate. She felt the Divine's spirit as she also felt the eyes of angels and did not want to leave the holy temple.

The Divine hand then draped her with a holy robe, which was dark blue with gold secret designs.

She felt safe within it. Wearing the robe, the Dreamer could be within the temple at all times. She wanted to stay there and asked the great gatekeeper if she could and He said, "Yes."

# Chapter Thirty Five

~

## *You Must Plant it*

Kneeling at the Divine's feet, the Dreamer waited for His word to write itself upon her tablet. The clouds of Heaven gently blew over her head and enveloped her in their cool warmth. Then He smiled at the Dreamer as He looked deep into her soul. He gave her a beautiful rose, deeply colored and very much alive. She bowed her head and gratefully accepted His gift. She felt the lifeblood pulsing within the rose as she held it in her hand. The bloom swayed and danced and then leaned into her.

The Divine said, "You must plant it."

The Dreamer put her writing tablet aside and held the rose in her lap thinking of where to plant it. She put the rose down for a moment to get something from her pocket, and as she did, the rose let out a small cry. Quickly, the Dreamer picked it up again and held it tenderly.

"I'm sorry, little rose. I won't put you down again," she said.

"You must plant it," repeated the Divine.

The Dreamer didn't understand what He wanted her to do, so she prayed. She clasped her hands around the bulb of the flower and its delicate aroma overcame her. It enveloped her and joined the clouds. The Divine smiled at her for He also held a rose in His hands. Her hands were soon covered in oil and the rose had grown roots, as she continued to pray.

"I do not understand this but I accept your bountiful gift," the Dreamer said, filled with gratitude. "I am humble before Thee and ask to be worthy to do your will and serve You."

She kept her eyes closed, but felt her robe changing form. She inhaled the perfume of the rose and wiped its oil on her face. When she opened her eyes, she saw that the rose had planted itself within her garment. Deep within her being, the Dreamer felt transformed. Her skin had become like the rose; her eyes could see things they could not before.

"I see that you have planted my rose, Dreamer," said the Divine. "Do you see that now it is you who must bloom?"

She thought for a moment. "Yes, I do."

"Good," said the Divine.

# Chapter Thirty Six

~

# *The Word*

The Dreamer awaited the word of the Divine, as she focused her attention on her breath.

The word was with the Divine until He gave it away, and then it came back to Him refreshed and restored. It left His lips and returned, but before it did, it traveled the world. All who read the word were transformed, and all who heeded it were saved, for the word was love.

The Divine spoke. "There is only one word and He has already come, yet He will come again. The word will one day again be spoken."

The Divine said, "Only those who are ready will hear the word. For I have hidden the word deep within the hearts of those who know. When the time is right, it is they who will speak and share it, and it is they who will honor it.

"Why so much pain, those who know have asked me. And I reply, it is not I who caused the pain, yet it is I who take it away. I cannot interfere, for long ago I gave mankind a gift of freedom, the freedom to choose. Once that gift was given, I could not take it back. I could not break a law I had created, and I could not take back a gift I had freely and lovingly given. Mankind must give that gift back to me, by choosing to love one another and me. Only when man chooses to love one another, chooses to come Home with me and to be one with the word will his pain end. Only then will the suffering cease."

# Chapter Thirty Seven

~

## *Reading the Fire*

Deep in meditation, the Dreamer was in the Divine's home surrounded by His presence, when she became aware of a great fire. She yearned to watch the fire and listen to it, so she walked towards it and sat down next to her mother who had earned the right to be there long ago. Ecstatic and embraced in one another's arms, together the Dreamer and her mother sat, reading the fire. They watched the fire dance and burn. Its color was bright with red and white heat. Then the Divine spoke to them and revealed many things.

"Children suffer," He said. "Parents cry. Women weep. Yet tears pass and they shape all spirits, carving the souls with their burning water. I know what burns within you, because I lit the fire within you long ago... the fire that brought you to me. This fire, the one you see before you, also burns within you. You feel it, don't you?"

The Dreamer looked at her mother, and in unison they answered, "We feel it within us, Father."

"Good," said the Divine, "because the fire is the only way Home. Put your hands within its flames."

The Dreamer and her mother looked at each other and reached deep into the flames with their hands. Immediately, the Dreamer's hands were cleansed and illuminated. Her mother's hands glowed, too. They smiled at one another.

The Divine explained, "Your hands have been blessed. Use them to do my work. Use them to heal and love one another. Cover your faces and feel my peace."

The women covered their faces with their hands and bowed their heads. The Dreamer felt His spirit take over her body and soul. She looked at her mother and knew the Divine's white heat filled her soul as well.

"Now," the Divine said, "step into the fire."

They stepped into the now purple fire but did not burn. The gold cross and chain the Dreamer had been wearing burned but did not melt. It scorched itself into her body but she did not feel pain. The Dreamer and her mother were transformed.

Then the Divine said, "Read the fire."

They opened their eyes and looked deep within the flames. The Dreamer saw her entire life, including her past and her future. Her mother also read her own life. They began to see the secrets of the universe, the beginning of the world, the creation of the sun, the movement of the stars, and the power of love that permeated it all. Love was the greatest force of all and lived within all things.

The Divine said, "Read the fire and remember what its flames tell you. The great fire burned its secrets deep within your soul. Remember this always."

Then, without knowing exactly when, the Dreamer awoke from her vision.

# Chapter Thirty Eight

~

## *The Master Carpenter*

The Dreamer sat beside the Mother as both watched the Master craft a long piece of wood. He was completely focused on the beam before Him.

"Watch him," the Mother said to the Dreamer.

The Dreamer studied Him as He caressed the wood with His left hand. In the center of the beam the Dreamer saw her face etching itself upon the smooth surface. He saw it too, and concentrated on the image of her face intensely. Then, the Master's brother appeared and saw the Dreamer's face in the wood too, and looked at her. The Master lovingly patted his brother on the back, smiled at him proudly, and encouraged him with love.

The Master could see His brother needed help with his own woodwork, and put His hands on the wood. Lost in concentration, the Master and His brother began to sculpt their wood. Beneath His touch the Dreamer's face and form began to come alive within the wood. The likeness was exact yet infused with something more, something special.

Any scraps that fell to the floor were putty in His hands as He molded them into life. The brother watched in amazement as the Master completed a carving of the Dreamer, a little smaller in size than she actually was. He held it in His hands as the

Dreamer, the Mother, and the brother all gazed upon it in awe. Then the Master blew upon it with His breath, and as He did, the Dreamer felt overcome with His spirit. He was the carpenter of her life.

He put the carving down by His feet in the tall grass of Heaven. Looking closely, the Dreamer could see thousands of carvings in the grass and knew these were all His children, created by His hands and by His breath.

The Dreamer looked at the brother and saw him deep in meditation upon his piece of wood. Then she saw the Master's face appear in the brother's wood and was mesmerized by it. Gently, the brother began to carve away the wood with his hands. The Master looked on lovingly, guiding His brother with His gaze. The form and face of the Master began to appear more clearly as they all held their breath.

Joy filled the brother's eyes and spirit as he saw the Master's image take form beneath his hands. When the brother finished his work, they all wept, for there before them stood the Master, carved with love in holy wood.

They were humble before the Master as the brother held the carving out to Him as a gift, as an offering. A great yet soft wind swept through the meadow they were in... the Divine breath. The carving came alive and light appeared in the beautifully etched eyes. Swept up by the wind, it flew into the hand of the Divine, who embraced the carving and held it to His heart.

"Whatever blood was once shed upon this wood," said the Master, "has now become a precious shrine. Yet the shrine is for the living, not the dead. And the wood is for the joyous, not the sorrowful. The faces carved here will be known in my kingdom. Happy are those who see their face among my meadow. No one can be placed here but by my hand. Always reach for my hand in your life and you will never be lost. Your heart will usually point the way. Listen to the leaves when they talk in the wind for they are leading you here."

The Dreamer saw a great and blinding omnipresent light. In that light the Dreamer saw millions of faces, carved in eternity, faces of grace and peace. She looked at her hands and wondered what she could create for Him. Invoking the heart of Heaven with her breath, she centered herself and searched her soul. She felt a beautiful pink rose bloom in the palms of her hands and knew she could create love with her hands and with her heart. She realized she would do this for Him. With this thought, more roses bloomed in her hands.

The Dreamer gave the Mother a rose and kissed Her hand, and then walked to the brother and patted his back. Tears filled his eyes when the Dreamer also gave him a holy rose.

Then the Master, His brother, the Mother, and the Dreamer gathered around one another and gave a prayer of thanks for the miracles they had witnessed and participated in. One by one, they each planted the Dreamer's roses in the grass of Heaven, which held the sacred carvings, and the roses took root and bloomed. To this day, their fragrance fills Heaven.

# Chapter Thirty Nine

~

## *There, Dreamer, There*

"There, Dreamer. Rest in my arms," said the Mother. "Think only of me and I will comfort you."

Her veil framed Her beautiful, radiant face. Her spirit burned from within and illuminated Her aura. She held the Dreamer's face in Her hands as She poured Her soul, love, and grace into the Dreamer.

She then took her by the hand and led her to a thorn bush. They looked at it for a moment, holding hands. She reached out and caressed it lovingly. The Dreamer didn't know what to do, so the Mother guided her hand and showed the Dreamer that she was to prick her finger. The Dreamer was afraid and didn't want to bleed, but she wanted to please and obey Her, and did as She asked. It hurt for just a moment and a radiant, deep rose blossomed in her palm. The Dreamer was delighted and held it out to Her as an offering.

The Mother nodded Her head in one direction and the Dreamer followed humbly behind Her as they walked towards a small running brook. Following Her, the Dreamer knelt beside the water and gave her rose to the stream. Her hands felt cool in the holy water. The Mother turned to the Dreamer and smiled. The water carried the Dreamer's rose down an eternal stream. It flowed beyond what her eyes could see, for as she looked down the river, she could see that her rose would travel forever. The Mother sat beside the Dreamer and held her hand.

"Do not miss the rose for its thorn will always be with you," She said. "Look at your hand. You are still bleeding yet you do not know it. Look at my hands."

Her hands were the purest, creamy white the Dreamer had ever seen. They were exquisite. Immaculate.

She said, "Come walk with me."

They walked for quite a way in silence. Serenity. They walked over hills and rocks, carefully placing their feet. Their heads were covered. They came to a hidden home, because it looked like it was part of a large tree trunk or rock. It was well cloaked by branches and grass and leaves. The Master had hidden it well, yet only the Mother knew where it was.

She parted the way for the Dreamer and opened the door, as she followed Her inside the tiny and sacred home. The one room had a simple wooden table in the middle with benches on either side. She sat down on one side while the Dreamer was led to sit down on the other. They held hands across the table and a large white, lit candle appeared on the table. She gazed deeply into the Dreamer's eyes locking her into Her presence.

"When I was a little girl," the Mother said, "people told me I was mad. Yet I knew better. I kept my silence and my prayers to myself. The Divine gave me All-knowing parents. I protected them well and they knew me.

"I had dreams, too, and always knew they would manifest. I never doubted for one minute, and learned a great deal in silence. All I needed to know I was taught in silence, and it is all there for you too, Dreamer."

The Mother stood and began to hang strings from

the beams in the ceiling, prayers from those who needed Her intercession. Each one She hung with great care, feeling the weeping of each soul who had cried out to Her. The Dreamer watched these strings as they swayed from Her touch. They were alive and they moved. As Her hand caressed them, tears fell from them. She continued to caress them with Her hand, and as She did, the floor began to flood.

Soon the Dreamer's feet were immersed in the tears of millions. She was overcome with grief and almost collapsed from the ache. She couldn't breathe, suffocated by the agony. The candle remained lit while its wax raced down the table to join the tears.

The Mother calmly walked around in a prayerful circle, humming and chanting Her prayer of love for humanity. She was peaceful, steady, righteous, and pure. The Dreamer knew by the look on Her face that She was with them...each one who had prayed to Her. In one moment She was with millions, and each one who felt Her thought She was there with them alone. Omnipresence.

The Dreamer put her hands on the wooden table and breathed deeply. Her hands began to radiate heat, feeling it from the table. She moved her left hand slightly and felt the stab of a splinter. She winced and looked up at the Mother, still lost in Her prayers. She opened Her eyes.

She spoke to the Dreamer, "Whenever there is a wound a rose will bloom, for wherever there is a wound, the doorway to eternity has been opened to you." Then the Mother closed Her eyes again.

The splinter traveled through the Dreamer's hand, up her arm to her heart. She felt it explode and her heart grew beyond her body, and transformed into a rose, with a hypnotic aroma. She felt weak yet strong.

The pool of tears reached to the Dreamer's knees

and she began to pray for those suffering. As she did, the pool began to subside. The Mother opened Her eyes and smiled at the Dreamer. She had been waiting for the Dreamer to help Her. The Dreamer stood up from the table and walked behind Her as She circled the room full of prayers. They walked around the room three times. When they eventually stopped in the center of the room, the tears were gone. The Mother looked at the Dreamer and held her face in Her hands. She thanked the Dreamer for her help.

"Mother," the Dreamer said, "I did nothing. You answered their prayers."

"Dreamer, you believed in me and loved them. You felt their pain. You showed me that you care deeply, which is an answer to my prayers."

Looking up at the ceiling, the Dreamer saw that the strings had fallen to the floor, and roses bloomed where the strings had fallen.

"Dreamer, always look up," the Mother said, "and there, you will find your answers."

They left the holy house and walked back to the thorn bush. While they were away, all the roses had blossomed completely and their aroma overwhelmed the Dreamer. She sat down by the bush beside the Mother. With her head on the Mother's lap, the Dreamer fell asleep, while the Mother caressed her hair.

Faintly, through the ears of almost sleep, the Dreamer heard the Mother say, "There, Dreamer, there."

# Chapter Forty

~

## Then She Spoke to Me

The Dreamer was walking through the clouds in Heaven. Her robe swayed in the wind. Then she came before the Mother and the Master and knelt in humility at their feet. They encircled her with their mighty power and infused her with their light.

The Mother said, "You were with me, Dreamer, when I gathered His belongings. You were with me when I wept and the weeping would not stop. And you were with me as an old woman, healing my wounds and tending to my needs."

The Dreamer looked at Her beautiful face, slowly remembering the time they had spent together.

"When I was crushed with grief, empty of my spirit, you carried me home and told me to believe," the Mother said. "You told me that the Divine would carry us through until we could see for ourselves. You and I were the first to witness, the first to lead the way. Others are still following where we led. Do not be afraid for I am with you."

The Dreamer was overcome, and knowing this, the Mother took the Dreamer's hand.

"Do you remember, Dreamer, how He came to tell us of His victory?" She asked.

Pausing for a moment, the Dreamer replied, "Yes, I do, Mother," reaching back through the pain in her heart. "I also remember the joy, the laughter, the pain, and the peace."

"Do you remember how He led us to gather all that belonged to Him... to the secret places where He had hidden His things?"

Memories began to flood the Dreamer's mind. She remembered quickly hunting for His things, searching so that His belongings would be righteously restored to His Mother. With each precious piece they found, they felt His presence and knew He was with them. All of His garments were returned to Her and this comforted Her greatly.

But nothing comforted Her more than to know that He had defeated death. Nothing healed Her grief more miraculously than His presence before Her, and of this the Dreamer was a witness to.

After being lost in thoughts, the Dreamer replied, "Mother, I remember."

The Dreamer remembered that the Mother gave her a robe of His, a piece of which she carried with her at all times. Still holding Her hand, the Mother poured Her love and grace into the Dreamer.

"Dear friend, you alone knew my grief then, yet you did not run away. For this, I will never leave you," the Mother said.

The Dreamer sobbed into Her hand and wiped her face in Her robe. In the Mother's free hand She held His cup, and began to gather the Dreamer's tears in it. Soon the cup was full, but her tears did not stop. They were tears of joy, not of sadness. She held the cup in Her hand for a moment and then placed it at the Master's feet when He appeared. The Dreamer could see there were many cups full of tears at the Master's feet. He knew every cup by name and guarded them. As He looked at the cup His Mother set before Him, the Dreamer's tears stopped forever.

# Chapter Forty One

~

## *The Hand That Never Let Go*

The Dreamer bowed before the Master and the Mother, and as her head was lowered, great boulders of salt fell upon the Dreamer's back. As they fell, they didn't hurt the Dreamer but fell apart and broke into pieces, in a soft shattering releasing their healing essence. The salt purified and cleansed the Dreamer.

Before her spread a glorious horizon and warm yellow light called the Dreamer forward. She walked on but seemed to take no steps. The light embraced her in its warmth, and she could no longer remember herself, for the Dreamer had become part of the light. She breathed in the light and exhaled love and light.

Gently, she felt a beautiful hand take hers, and the Dreamer felt a pull on her soul. She was swiftly led through the clouds to a place she had not been before, yet somehow knew. Purple light floated through the air and swirled around her. There was a gentle rain of gemstones. As the gems fell, they blanketed the floor with their brilliant light that bounced from each reflection the Dreamer looked at.

Then she saw gold veins threaded through all of the fallen gems, linking them in a glorious tapestry. The Dreamer reached to touch them and her hands sunk into the gems. They felt cool to the touch, yet their vibration was electric. The hand that joined hers also rested in the gems that lay on the ground of Heaven. All that was precious lived there. The Dreamer was so happy there, as all that she loved lived there.

She lay on the lawn of gems, and as she did, the hand that held hers did the same. The Dreamer was immersed within the gold and gems. The purple and white light still floated within the wind and gently flew through her. The Dreamer was at peace and completely at rest, because the hand that held hers never let go.

# Chapter Forty Two

~

# *The Scroll*

In her left hand the Dreamer held a tall wooden staff the Master had given her, that would later become a sword. She was also wearing a robe He had given her, dressed in His armor ready to fight the good fight. She knew she would defend Him with her life, but death was not what He was asking of her. What He was asking was life, love, honor, and fortitude.

He held in His hand an ancient scroll tied with soft leather. The paper was ancient and its edges were worn. Cautiously He unrolled it and stopped at the passage He wanted to read to the Dreamer. He spoke the words almost in a whisper.

"Great are all things in my Father's house. Splendid are all who dwell here for they know the way in. He who does not knock will find no answer. He who waits at the door patiently will have all doors opened. Even I cannot open all doors, but my Father before me can. For He is the one who built them.

"All jewels and riches are here, and are happiest here. It pains them to leave and journey elsewhere, even if it is for a short time. You are like those jewels... precious, tiny, and glistening. You, too, are unhappy anywhere but here. You, too, have searched your whole life looking for your perfect home. As these jewels are happiest only in my Father's throne, so are you happiest in His Home.

"Dreamer, you must first remember where you come from, for if you know where you belong, no journey will ever be too far or too long.

"Never lose your vision. Others will try to steal it from you so you must keep it sacred and hidden at all times. Cloak it so that others may not see what you see, and you will never be lost.

"Finally, you must never give up hope for hope is the carrier of faith. In all circumstances, believe."

The Master looked at the Dreamer and rolled up the ancient scroll. She wanted to hear more, and knowing her every thought, He looked at her and said, "Another time, Dreamer... another time."

If you would like to contact Sonya Haramis, M.Ed. or order additional books, please visit:
www.peaceofthedreamer.com

Blessings, Love, and Light!

125